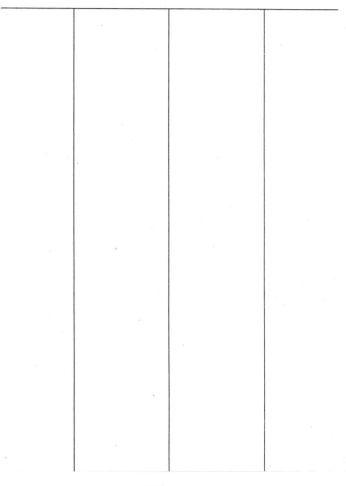

Editor

Craig Donnellan

First published by Independence
PO Box 295
Cambridge CB1 3XP
England

British Library Cataloguing in Publication Data
Fertility Rights – (Issues Series)
I. Donnellan, Craig II. Series
612.6

ISBN 1 86168 140 2

Printed in Great Britain
The Burlington Press
Cambridge

Typeset by
Claire Boyd

Cover
The illustration on the front cover is by
Pumpkin House.

CONTENTS

Introduction

Fertility Rights is the eleventh volume in the **Issues** series. The aim of this series is to offer up-to-date information about important issues in our world.

Fertility Rights looks at the causes of infertility, the treatments, and the ethical issues.

The information comes from a wide variety of sources and includes:
Government reports and statistics
Newspaper reports and features
Magazine articles and surveys
Literature from lobby groups
and charitable organisations.

It is hoped that, as you read about the many aspects of the issues explored in this book, you will critically evaluate the information presented. It is important that you decide whether you are being presented with facts or opinions. Does the writer give a biased or an unbiased report? If an opinion is being expressed, do you agree with the writer?

Fertility Rights offers a useful starting-point for those who need convenient access to information about the many issues involved. However, it is only a starting-point. At the back of the book is a list of organisations which you may want to contact for further information.

*****

What can cause infertility?

Information from fpa (formerly The Family Planning Association)

Fertility problems may occur in men or women and several things can affect your chances of a successful pregnancy.

Causes of infertility and possible treatments

- A woman who has difficulty in ovulating may need a course of drugs.
- A woman not producing eggs may need another woman to donate eggs (this is not routinely offered).
- A woman with blocked Fallopian tubes may need surgery or assisted conception.
- A man with low numbers and/or poor quality sperm may need assisted conception to aid fertilisation using his own sperm. Or sperm from a donor may be needed.

There may be other, less common, causes and a couple may have a combination of problems, so investigations need to be completed even if one problem is found at an early stage. Most problems can be helped, with varying degrees of success. Sometimes, even after full investigations, the reason for infertility cannot be found but assisted conception treatment may still be successful.

Obtaining treatment

Visiting your GP gives you and your partner the opportunity to ask about the possible investigations and treatments, waiting lists and any costs. You can then decide if you want to go ahead with tests and/or treatment. You will want to know what treatments are offered locally on the NHS and, if you wish to consider paying for private treatment, what private treatments are available locally. You should also find out if your GP will meet the costs of any prescribed drugs or if you will have to pay for them.

While GPs can do some preliminary investigations, you may need to be referred to a specialist fertility clinic. If so, you will need a referral letter from your GP. The provision of specialist services within the NHS is limited in some areas and waiting lists vary for certain types of treatment, so try and find out how long you will have to wait for an appointment.

Eligibility for NHS treatment

The type of treatment you can receive on the NHS depends on a number of factors, including what infertility services individual health authorities decide they will purchase.

Some patients will be investigated and treated only at their local District General Hospital, others may be referred on to a specialist unit. There is often a limit on the amount of treatment you can receive.

While most tests and investigations are carried out on the NHS, around 80% of in-vitro fertilisation (IVF) treatment is carried out privately. You need to find out what the funding and selection criteria are to see if you will be eligible for NHS treatment. Your GP, practice nurse or your local Community Health Council (CHC) will be able to help you with this. You can find your CHC in the phone book. You could also contact the Human Fertilisation and Embryology Authority for a copy of its *Patients' Guide* to clinics.

You can seek treatment as a private and NHS patient at the same time if you have a separate referral letter from your GP for each option. You need to be aware that some health authorities may not fund NHS treatment if you have already had similar treatment on a private basis.

The National Infertility Awareness Campaign has useful information for people who have funding problems.

Tests and investigations

The kind of tests that are done vary from clinic to clinic and all of the following may not be necessary as one or two may give a diagnosis. Once you have a diagnosis fairly simple treatment or surgery may be all that is needed.

Tests for a man may involve:

- Semen analysis to look at the number, shape and size of sperm and how well they move. More than one test should be carried out.
- Blood or urine tests to check hormone levels.
- Testing the sperm in special solutions.
- Special X-rays/scans to find blockages or check blood supply to the testes.

Where sperm counts stay low or are absent, assisted conception may be effective.

Tests for women may involve:

- Blood, urine and cervical mucus checks to check hormone levels or ovulation.
- Ultrasound scans to check if a follicle, which should contain an egg, is being produced.

Treatment for ovulation problems usually involves drugs – by tablets, injections or nasal inhalations – and has a high success rate if the correct diagnosis has been established.

- Sperm mucus crossover – this checks if the woman's cervical mucus allows her partner's sperm through.
- Endometrial biopsy – a tiny sample of womb lining (endometrium) is removed to check that it is free from infection and that ovulation has occurred.
- An hysterosalpingogram where dye is passed through the Fallopian tubes to check that they are open and clear of obstruction.
- A laparoscopy (usually under general anaesthetic) uses a thin telescope-like instrument to view the reproductive organs through a small cut below the navel. It checks for scar tissue, endometriosis, fibroids or any abnormality in the shape or position of the womb, ovaries or Fallopian tubes. At the same time a dye may be passed through the Fallopian tubes to see if they are open and clear.

Assisted conception techniques

Assisted conception techniques have been used successfully for many years and a range of techniques are available. It is now possible for some men with very low sperm counts or

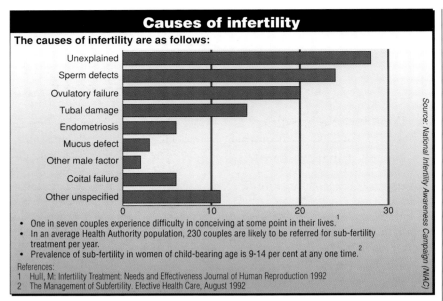

Source: National Infertility Awareness Campaign (NIAC)

even with no sperm in their semen to have their own genetic children. A specialist clinic will be able to advise you on which treatment will be best for you.

The most well-known treatment is in-vitro fertilisation (IVF), in which eggs are removed from the woman, fertilised in the laboratory and the embryo is then placed into her womb. Donor insemination (DI) uses sperm from anonymous donors where there are severe problems with the man's sperm. Gamete Intra-Fallopian Transfer (GIFT) uses a couple's own eggs and sperm, or that of donors, which are mixed together and placed in the woman's Fallopian tubes where they fertilise. Intra-cytoplasmic Sperm Injection (ICSI) uses a single sperm injected into the woman's egg which is then transferred to the womb after fertilisation.

These are not miracle solutions. The age of the woman is very important and someone aged under 35 has a much better chance of a successful pregnancy than a woman over 40.

Donor insemination (DI) of sperm and donor eggs

If a man produces no or few normal sperm, carries an inherited disease, or has had a vasectomy, then insemination using sperm from an anonymous donor may be considered. Egg donation may be an option if a woman is not producing eggs or has a genetic problem. The decision to use donor sperm or eggs can be a difficult one. You can get

help in making this decision from a counsellor or support group.

Clinics that offer this service have to send information about donors, recipients and the outcome of treatment to the HFEA. Donors have to meet extensive screening criteria, including HIV testing. A man may not usually donate sperm after ten live births have resulted from his semen donations. Donors do not have to be anonymous and most clinics will accept a donor that a couple has found for themselves.

Counselling and support

Couples report that the many hospital visits needed and the time spent waiting between treatments to learn if each stage has worked is stressful. All units providing IVF and other licensed conception techniques have a legal responsibility to offer counselling. Counselling can allow you to talk through what the treatment entails and how you feel about it, and can give support during the process and if the treatment fails.

If you don't want to see a counsellor at the clinic you are attending, the British Infertility Counsellors Association can put you in touch with your nearest infertility counsellor. Some people find being in contact with others in a similar situation or with a support group helps them through infertility. You can contact CHILD, The National Fertility Support Network or ISSUE, The National Fertility Association for details of your nearest one.

© fpa

Male infertility

Information from PPP healthcare

What is male infertility?

The definition of infertility is when a couple have not conceived after 12-18 months of unprotected intercourse. For approximately 40% of cases at least part of the problem involves the male who, for a variety of reasons, is unable to produce an ejaculate containing sufficient numbers of normal functioning sperm which will pass through the female tract and fertilise the egg.

In the healthy male, sperms are produced in large numbers in the testes and are stored in a system of coiled tubes situated behind the testicle, called the epididymis. During ejaculation, they pass through a tube (the vas) and out through the urethra towards the tip of the penis. Sperm reside within the body for about three months from the time the sperm are made to the point at which they are released at ejaculation.

In order to fertilise the partner's egg, the sperms which are deposited in the vagina need to penetrate the neck of the womb and pass up the cavity to meet the egg previously released from the ovary. In a normal ejaculate, up to 100 million sperms or more are released.

Why does it occur?

Male infertility, therefore, involves a problem of both quantity and quality of the sperm in that they need to be able to swim by themselves to meet the partner's egg and then be healthy enough to fertilise it. Male infertility exists if the sperm containing fluid (seminal fluid) contains either no sperm (azoospermia), too few sperm (oligospermia) or too high a proportion of abnormal sperm.

How does it occur?

There may be several potential causes of failed egg penetration:
- Obstruction to sperm transport: Obstruction could occur between the testes and the urethra, due most often to inflammation of the epididymis. Such infection may lead to scarring and blockage of the tube. Obstruction sometimes follows surgery, such as hernia repair, or rarely there may be a congenital absence of the vas, so transport of sperm is physically impossible.
- Varicocele: This is a swelling of the veins of the testicle (similar to varicose veins) and affects sperm production.
- Mumps: If this occurs after puberty the testis may be affected (due to inflammation – orchitis) and this can reduce the sperm count.
- Immunological factors: The body can falsely recognise sperm as being 'foreign' and develop antibodies to its own sperm; these may impair the ability of the sperm to penetrate the female cervical mucus.
- Impotence: Failed erection will naturally impair ejaculation and several potential causes exist such as diabetes, excess alcohol, and drugs such as beta blockers and diuretics.
- Other physical agents: Some occupations are associated with environmental factors which reduce male fertility by impairing sperm formation. Such related factors include excessive heat, exposure to lead and other heavy metals, insecticides and excessive smoking and alcohol intake. Exposure to x-rays and any chronic severe illness can depress the sperm count. It may take 3-6 months for recovery of sperm function after such an illness.
- Genetic causes: This occurs rarely and is due to Kleinfelters Syndrome where the male is born with an extra x chromosome in their genetic make-up and as a result produces no sperm.
- Hormonal causes: In some cases insufficient levels of hormone necessary for sperm production may be produced or the testis itself may, through a hormone deficiency, be small or even absent.

What are the tests?

Semen analysis is the main investigation. The man should abstain from intercourse for 3-4 days

before collecting a specimen for analysis which should be obtained by masturbation and collected in a sterile container. It is important not to use a condom in collecting a sample as the rubber destroys the sperm. A semen analysis will give the following data:

- Volume to more than 2ml
- Density. Usually in excess of 60 million sperm per millilitre is normal
- Morphology (or shape and appearance) of sperm. 75% should be of normal form
- Anti-sperm antibodies. These may cause sperm to clump together and thus impede their ability to swim along to reach and fertilise the egg

What is the treatment?

Treatment is available but success cannot be guaranteed. In all cases treatment of underlying causes is the main aim.

Stopping smoking and reducing alcohol intake are advisable as these can both impede sperm production. Checking of the male hormone (testosterone) level is important as hormone injection treatment may be necessary every 2-4 weeks. Results may however be disappointing. Where hormone levels are normal and no sperm production is evident then the search for a tubal blockage may be indicated especially where there has been previous surgery.

Exploration of the testicle sac (the scrotum) is done under a general anaesthetic and the surgeon will look for an obstruction which may require an x-ray (a vasogram). A blocked vas may require a bypass operation. A varicocele may be removed surgically and this may restore fertility. Where anti-sperm anti-bodies are present the use of steroids (cortisone) will, by their anti-inflammatory effect, occasionally restore fertility.

Artificial insemination: Where sperm counts stay low then either artificial insemination by the husband (AIH) or by a donor (AID) can help. If the count is too low for AIH or for assisted conception (see below) then AID will be considered. Although effective as

a solution, the decision to accept this method can present social and moral difficulties for some men and careful counselling of the couple may be necessary.

Assisted conception: In-vitro fertilisation (IVF) is suitable in cases where there are low numbers of motile (active) but otherwise normal sperms. Because IVF results in the sperm being placed in immediate contact with the egg, fertilisation can be achieved with very low numbers of motile sperm. However the success rates from IVF treatment are lower when there is a male problem.

There are now methods of sperm preparation in which a concentration of motile sperm can be achieved from an otherwise low sperm population. Chemical stimulants are now being used to improve motility of defective sperm and are being used in conjunction with IVF. Micromanipulation techniques have concentrated on making it easier for defective sperm to penetrate the female egg. Success rates are currently low and research is still in progress.

Where can I get further information?

Apart from contacting your GP, the following organisations may be of further help:
CHILD Self Help Support Group, Charter House, 43 St Leonards Road, Bexhill on Sea, East Sussex. Telephone: 01424 732361. Email: mailto:office@email2.child.org.uk
Web page: http://www.child.org.uk
Family Planning Association, 2-12 Pentonville Road, London, N1 9FP. Helpline: 020 7837 4044 (9.00-19.00 Mon-Fri)

Sources
1. Bobak, A. (1995) Infertility.Part 1. *GP Medicine*, 30th June 1995
2. Klass, E.J., Reitelman, C. (1995) Adolescent varicocele. *Urological Clinics of North America*, 22(1) pp.151-159
3. Ohl, D.A., Mas, R.K. (1995) Infertility due to antisperm antibodies. *Urology*, 46(4) pp.591-602

Female infertility

Information from PPP healthcare

What is female infertility?

The definition of infertility is when a couple have not conceived after 12 -18 months of unprotected intercourse. Normally, after one year of trying 95% of normal fertile couples will have conceived. Infertility is said to affect about 1 in 7 couples in the UK.

Why does it occur?

In about one in four of all couples investigated for infertility, no definite diagnosis can be reached and one can only refer to this as 'unexplained' infertility. Women generally become less fertile as they get older and as couples delay starting a family until much later so the treatment may be correspondingly less successful.

How does it occur?

The main causes of infertility in women are the following :

Failure of ovulation: This occurs when the ovaries fail to produce eggs each month and can be due to a problem within the ovary itself, for example, when the ovary has developed many cysts within it (polycystic disease). Alternatively there may be a hormonal cause where the chemical messengers produced in the brain's master gland (the hypothalamus) do not provide the correct hormones to trigger off ovulation in the ovary. The functioning of the hypothalamus can be affected by outside factors such as severe dieting, chronic stress and chronically poor nutrition which in turn can affect the ability to ovulate.

Blocked Fallopian tubes: These are very delicate complex structures which transport eggs, sperm and early embryos. They can become narrowed or blocked by scar tissue formed as a result of inflammation within the tubes. This prevents fertilisation and embryo transport. If only one tube is blocked the woman may still be fertile but it may take longer to achieve a pregnancy.

Tubal disease: This may occur due to adhesions or 'bands of scar tissue' caused by previous surgery or infection. These may 'kink' the tubes and so prevent egg transport. Specific infection with an organism called chlamydia can cause pelvic inflammatory disease which can disturb normal function of the tubes.

Endometriosis: Damage can be caused to the ovary, tubes, or other organs in the pelvic area when endometrial tissue (which is normally confined to the lining of the uterus) grows outside the uterus, and damages these organs and affects ability to conceive.

Fibroids: These are benign fibrous growths occurring outside, within, or inside the wall of the uterus which can interfere with implantation of the embryo.

Failure of fertilisation and implantation: This can occur if the body produces special proteins (antibodies) which render the sperm less motile (active) and therefore less able to fertilise the egg.

Problems with intercourse: This may be because the male is impotent or alternatively it may arise because intercourse itself is painful for the woman (because of a physical problem) and therefore an unpleasant experience. This may cause fear and the associated anxiety can prevent a couple from relaxing

What are the tests?

Investigations usually commence when the woman has tried unsuccessfully to become pregnant after

---

In about one in four of all couples investigated for infertility, no definite diagnosis can be reached and one can only refer to this as 'unexplained' infertility

---

18-24 months of unprotected intercourse and these can be initiated by the family doctor.

Ovulation: Some doctors ask women to keep a temperature chart for 3-6 months. A mid cycle temperature 'spike' indicates ovulation. This can be accompanied by a blood test to check the serum progesterone hormone level at day 21 of the cycle. If the level is sufficiently high on this day then this indicates satisfactory ovulation.

Post coital test: Cervical mucus is taken from the vagina around the time of ovulation and about 8 hours after intercourse. The mucus is examined under a microscope for evidence of satisfactory sperm activity.

Investigation of mucus: Cervical mucus is present throughout the menstrual cycle but greatly increases in quantity at ovulation. Mucus taken at ovulation is placed in contact with the male sperm to check whether the mucus prevents sperm penetration.

Endometrial biopsy: A tiny sample of the womb lining (endometrium) is taken to check if it has responded to hormonal cycle changes and is free from infection.

Assessment of tubal patency: A telescope instrument is inserted into the abdomen through a small cut made beneath the navel (laparoscopy). This procedure can establish if scar tissue, fibroids or other anatomical problems are affecting the womb, ovary, or fallopian tubes. By passing a blue dye through the tubes (hydrotubation) blockages in the tubes can be discovered. An ultrasound scan can assess the shape of the uterus and establish any physical abnormality.

What is the treatment?

The type of treatment will vary according to the underlying cause, but in all cases this should be part of a shared programme between the doctor and the couple.

Ovarian failure: Treatment with a special drug (clomiphene) will help, by stimulating ovulation. Fifty per cent of women will become pregnant within six months. The tablet is taken on day 2-5 of each cycle.

Tubal blockage: This can be corrected surgically, but success is more usual in women with only minor tubal damage.

Endometriosis: This may be treated surgically if confined to the fallopian tube but if it is widespread in the pelvis then a hormone treatment (with a drug called danazol) for a 6-9-month period will help cure the problem.

Assisted conception: Couples who are not suitable or who have been unsuccessful with other methods may be offered assisted conception (known as IVF or GIFT).

- In-vitro fertilisation (IVF): The ovaries are artifically stimulated by hormones and (under scan control in an IVF unit) several eggs are collected or harvested. After fertilisation outside the womb, 3-4 eggs are transferred back into the womb for attempted implantation. Pregnancy rates for IVF from established centres approach 30% per cycle and birth rates of around 25% per cycle can now be expected in women under 40 years old (assuming that the sperm function of the partner is normal).

- Gamete infusion (GIFT): Sperm and egg are transferred into the fallopian tube where fertilisation and implantation occur naturally.

These techniques are not simple and several attempts may be needed as assisted conception does not always result in pregnancy. Full counselling by the doctors is very important as the programme may be stressful to the couple especially if several failed attempts occur.

Where can I get further information?

Apart from contacting your GP, the following organisations may be of further help:

Family Planning Association, 2-12 Pentonville Road, London, N1 9FP. Helpline: 020 7837 4044 (9.00-19.00 Mon-Fri)

CHILD Self Help Support Group, Charter House, 43 St Leonards Road, Bexhill on Sea, East Sussex. Telephone: 01424 732361. Email: mailto:office@email2.child.org.uk Web site: www.child.org.uk

Sources
1. Shushan, A., Eisenberg, V.H., Schenker, J.G. (1995) Sub-fertility in the era of assisted reproduction. *Fertility and Sterility*, 64(3) pp.459-69
2. Marshall, K., Senior, J., Clayton, J. (1996) Womens Health: 2. Infertility. *Pharmaceutical Journal*, 256(6881) pp.303-307

Fertility myths

The following fertility myths have kindly been produced by Professor William Ledger MA, DPhil MRCOG from the Jessop Hospital For Women UK

Introduction

Since one in seven couples seek medical advice to achieve a pregnancy, infertility and its causes are an everyday concern for many couples in the UK. It is very rare that a month passes without the media publicising some new opinion or theory about the cause of infertility and a subsequent solution – yet a great many myths still exist about infertility, its causes and its treatment.

There is no doubt that stress, overwork, obesity, smoking and over-consumption of alcohol along with little understanding about the reproductive cycle can cause problems for many couples, but in many cases we must not lose sight of the fact that clinical problems do exist. In the following chapters, we have tried to explain many of the misconceptions surrounding the biological and clinical aspects of infertility.

Modern infertility treatment is successful – the chances of conceiving in one cycle of infertility treatment can be up to 25 per cent. In the great confusion that surrounds infertility it is easy to forget that even for normal fertile couples, the chance of getting pregnant in any one month is only about 25 per cent. On average, it will take the same couple approximately seven months to conceive.

When you consider that for one cycle of in-vitro fertilisation (IVF) the success rate can be up to 25 per cent, it follows that the more cycles of treatment a couple have the greater their chances of achieving conception. However, it is often the delays in receiving NHS funded treatment that reduce a couple's chances of success and this not only wastes valuable time for patients but valuable NHS resources.

General infertility

Infertility is a woman's problem

Infertility is a medical problem that can be related to the man, the woman or both. Approximately 35 per cent of cases are due to a female problem, 35 per cent due to a male problem and in the rest of the cases the causes are unexplained. It is essential that both men and women are investigated. Until recently, attention was centred on the female reproductive system. However, research has shown that many problems relate to men – for example, declining sperm counts, increased incidence of sperm and testicular abnormalities and decreased libido have all been cited as reasons for a couple's failure to conceive. Consequently, most of the new solutions are aimed at men.

You are less of a man because you can't father a child

A man's level of fertility is not a measure of how masculine he is. Infertility is a medical condition just like arthritis or asthma, which requires medical treatment.

Infertility is on the increase

There is no real evidence to suggest that this is the case. It is possible that we are simply more aware of it and couples who are experiencing infertility are more inclined to seek the increasing amount of help that is available to them. Many women are deciding to wait longer (until their mid-thirties) to have children. As a woman gets older, her reproductive capabilities begin to decrease. Until recently, there was not much that could be done for couples with infertility problems. However, now there are numerous assisted conception treatments available. It is difficult to link declining birth rates to infertility as many other factors are involved. Birth rates are also decided by social factors such as the population's outlook for the future – recession, career and education.

Infertility caused by blocked tubes is due to contracting a sexually transmitted disease at an early age

Although one of the causes of blocked tubes is the contraction of a sexually transmitted disease, Chlamydia, there are a number of other medical conditions, for example, appendicitis, endometriosis, and pelvic inflammatory disease, which can cause a blockage to occur.

Women who don't have periods cannot have children

Approximately one per cent of women in the UK suffer from premature menopause. These women can be helped to have children through infertility treatment, usually using donated eggs. Many women who do not have periods are not necessarily experiencing the menopause – periods can stop because of excessive weight gain or loss, extreme exercise regimes, or hormonal imbalances. Most women with these problems can be helped to conceive without too much difficulty

Sexual intercourse

There are many myths surrounding sexual intercourse and the best time to conceive.

Coital position affects the chance of conception

There are many myths surrounding sexual intercourse and the best time to conceive. Many couples widely believe that the position taken during sexual intercourse will affect their chances of getting pregnant. Further-

more, many believe their chances of conceiving are increased by lying on their backs for 20 minutes, ensuring the semen stays in the neck of the uterus for longer.

Whilst semen does inevitably come out of the vagina following ejaculation, sufficient sperm are deposited in the neck of the womb and are able to begin their journey towards the egg, regardless of the position taken.

Potency is improved by 'saving up' semen through infrequent intercourse

Millions of sperm are produced every day in the testicles. The sperm are stored in a tiny sac, the epididymis, which lies at the top of each testicle. Abstaining from sex in order to accumulate sperm so that more are deposited at the neck of the womb will not increase your chances of achieving conception, in fact the stored, older sperm may be of inferior quality and even hinder the newly produced, healthier sperm from reaching the egg.

Low level libido or failure of female orgasm inhibits conception

There is no evidence to support this statement. Furthermore, a woman does not need to achieve an orgasm in order to conceive.

Over-the-counter preparations or supplements can increase sperm count

There are no credible data to support this claim, although some

preparations and supplements may improve your overall feeling of well being.

Cold baths and loose pants can improve potency

The testicles are located outside a man's body to ensure successful maturation of the sperm, which takes place at a temperature about 30C lower than that of the rest of the body. In addition to their vulnerable position, the tissue surrounding the testicles contains little or no fat, affording no protection from the external environment. In short, look after them – they are fragile organs.

According to the Royal College of Obstetricians and Gynaecologists' (RCOG) *Evidence based clinical guidelines*, men with poor sperm quality are advised to avoid occupational or social situations that might cause the temperature in the testicles to rise. They recommend these men should avoid having hot baths or wearing tight fitting underwear and trousers if at all possible.

Infertility treatment

Infertility treatment is not a health need

In general, the majority of couples worldwide choose to start a family either as a conscious decision or by accident, whilst infertile couples are denied this most fundamental life choice. Many things can go wrong with the male and female reproductive system, either before birth or during their lifetime, such as dysfunctional sperm or blocked tubes – all of which can prevent them from starting a family.

Infertility means a total absence of reproductive function and this is very rare. Most couples are subfertile, which means that biologically parts of their reproductive system are impaired, resulting in a reduced chance of conceiving. Many of these couples can be helped by medical intervention and with the aid of the advanced reproductive technology that is available. Involuntary childlessness should rank as one of life's greatest traumas and causes immense pain and suffering. It is unfair to classify infertile couples as undeserving recipients of medical treatment.

Fertility treatment is experimental and children conceived by assisted conception techniques have an increased risk of developing abnormalities

Infertility treatment makes some people feel incredibly uncomfortable because they fear that scientists are playing God, or trying to alter the course of nature. However, infertility treatment has been the focus of much scientific research for over 200 years, with the first successful artificial insemination of a woman with her husband's sperm taking place in the late 1700s . One of the most significant landmarks in the modern history of reproductive technology was the birth of Louise Brown in 1978 – the first test-tube baby.

Many children conceived by assisted conception techniques have now reached adulthood and are leading perfectly normal, healthy lives. Fertility therapy has expanded more than any other field of medicine over the last decade and the treatments offered by clinicians are part of a long and continuous process of enquiry. The Human Fertilisation and Embryology Authority (HFEA) is a statutory body that regulates, licenses and collects data on fertility treatments such as in-vitro fertilisation (IVF) and donor insemination (DI) as well as human embryo research in the UK. Furthermore, the HFEA monitors all UK clinics that store eggs, sperm or embryos and offer IVF or DI to ensure that they conform to high medical and professional standards. Over 100,000 IVF children have been born worldwide and careful follow-up studies in a number of countries have failed to detect any deviation from normal development.

Infertility drugs can cause cancer

The link between fertility drugs and ovarian cancer has been the subject of much intense research. However, although it is possible that infertile women are at a greater risk of developing ovarian cancer, regardless of whether they have had infertility treatment, the consensus view is that it remains unproven.

Fertility treatment does not work

Modern assisted conception techniques are successful and have helped thousands of couples have the children they longed for and will no doubt assist many more in the future.

The chance of getting pregnant in one cycle of infertility treatment can be up to 25 per cent and this compares very favourably with natural conception in fertile couples, which can also be up to 25 per cent in any one month. It follows that the more treatment cycles an infertile couple can have, the greater the chance they have of achieving conception. Furthermore, the chances of conceiving through infertility treatment have steadily increased in the past few years due to the introduction of newer, more effective drugs and procedures. These improvements have also made fertility treatment less unpleasant and hence less stressful for couples.

Using donor eggs and sperm may cause future problems if our children want to know their biological origins
When couples undergo infertility treatment they will be faced with many issues and these will not just relate to the medical procedures involved in the treatment. If donor eggs and sperm are used, couples need to be clear in their minds about all the potential ramifications of successful treatment and be aware of the issues they may have to confront.

At present, only non-identifying information about a donor is disclosed to a couple following treatment with donated sperm and eggs. The 1990 Human Fertilisation and Embryology Authority Act specifically prevents the disclosure of any identifying information and the names relating to all current and past donors to the offspring. However, the HFEA does collect additional information about donors because it may allow the children to gain some insight into their genetic origins.

Several companies have started advertising sperm donors on the Internet and it is possible to obtain donor sperm for a few hundred pounds. There are serious potential dangers from obtaining sperm in this way. There is no guarantee that the sperm will have undergone the necessary rigorous screening for diseases such as HIV, syphilis or hepatitis. There is no way of ensuring that the sperm is of good enough quality to achieve fertilisation or that it belongs to the man advertised. Women should be aware that under UK common law, the donor of sperm obtained other than from HFEA licensed centres may be considered to be the legal father of any child born as a result of treatment. The HFEA encourages all women considering DI to contact a UK licensed clinic.

Ovulation
There is much confusion surrounding ovulation and the best time to have sexual intercourse in order to achieve conception.

The ovaries alternate each month
Ovulation is an entirely random process and eggs are not necessarily released from alternate ovaries each month. However, if you only have one functioning ovary, you will usually ovulate every month from that ovary. Clinicians are only able to predict which ovary is going to ovulate on approximately the eighth day of the cycle when the follicle containing the egg can be seen with ultrasound scanning.

If you're having periods, you are ovulating
Just because you have menstruated does not necessarily mean you have ovulated. However, if you are having regular periods at monthly intervals, it is more likely that ovulation is taking place.
• The above is an extract from www.ein.org
© *Professor William Ledger MA*

More couples beat male infertility

A treatment for male infertility is helping more couples to have babies of their own, figures revealed yesterday.

The Human Fertilisation & Embryology Authority said that treatments with 'ICSI', used when the male partner has too few and low quality sperm, have increased by 30 per cent. At the same time use of donor insemination, using another man's sperm, the main clinical solution for male infertility for decades, has fallen by 11 per cent.

The annual report of the HFEA says that in the year to March 1998, a total of 26,685 women received test-tube baby treatment which resulted in 6,864 pregnancies and 5,687 babies born, a live birth rate of 16.4 per cent. All fertility treatments resulted in 7,397 babies born in the year under review.

By Celia Hall, Medical Editor

The ICSI procedure, Intra Cytoplasmic Sperm Injection, which selects the most active sperm and injects it directly into the egg, was provided 9,295 times compared to 6,652 in the previous year with a birth rate of 20.7 per cent. Ruth

In 1998 a total of 26,685 women received test-tube baby treatment which resulted in 6,864 pregnancies and 5,687 babies born, a live birth rate of 16.4 per cent

Deech, chairman of the HFEA, said: 'ICSI has enabled men who in the past would not have been able to have children of their own, to do so.

'The HFEA continues to inspect licensed clinics offering this treatment to ensure that patients receive the highest standard of care and medical expertise.' The use of ICSI has grown steadily. In 1991 only 80 treatments took place. By 1995 when the number had risen to more than 1,500 the authority introduced checks on the competency of doctors as 'success is largely dependent on the skill and experience of its practioners'.

The number of patients seeking fertility treatment has risen steadily from 14,997 in 1992-93 to 26,690 in 1997-98. Experts say that one in seven couples have problems becoming pregnant.
© *Telegraph Group Limited, London 2000*

Fertility laws

By Mark Tran

Why is fertility in the news?

The Human Fertilisation and Embryology Authority (HFEA) is bracing itself for legal challenges from single women, older women and gay men who believe existing fertility rules in the UK have denied them the right to have children. Ruth Deech, the head of the HFEA, told the *Guardian* that European human rights legislation which comes into effect in the autumn could lead to test cases over fertility issues.

What is the HFEA?

The HFEA was set up in August 1991 by the Human Fertilisation and Embryology Act 1990 (HFE Act). The first statutory body of its type in the world, the HFEA was created to regulate a sensitive area amid public and professional unease about human embryo research and infertility treatments. HFEA members are appointed by the government. The recommendation for such a body had come from the 1984 report of the committee of inquiry into human fertilisation and embryology (the 'Warnock' report). In practical terms, the HFEA ensures that all UK treatment clinics offering in-vitro fertilisation (IVF) or donor insemination, or storing eggs, sperm or embryos, conform to high medical and professional standards and are inspected regularly.

What are the HFEA's main rules or recommendations on fertility treatment?

The HFEA produces a code of practice to guide licensed clinics. The code includes a key section on welfare of the child. While the offer of treatment is a decision ultimately for the patient's clinician, the HFE Act requires every clinician to make this decision only after 'account has been taken of the welfare of any child who may be born as a result of the treatment (including the need of that child for a father), and of any other child who may be

affected by the birth'. Clinics must bear in mind factors such as the prospective parents' ages and their likely future ability to look after, or provide for, a child's needs, and any risk of harm to the child or children who may be born. Where the child will have no legal father, clinics must pay particular attention to the prospective mother's ability to meet the child's needs throughout its childhood.

So where do the problems come in?

In practice, single women, gay women and older women have little chance of being treated in private clinics on the NHS, where budgets for IVF are tight. NHS clinics usually do not select people who are over 40, or even in their late 30s, and who are not part of a stable heterosexual couple.

Why should this lead to lawsuits?

Ruth Deech believes that European human rights legislation being introduced could open the door for lawsuits in Britain. The human rights legislation was originally a response to Nazi atrocities, to make sure there would never be a repeat of forced sterilisation of men and women. European legislation includes provisions on the right to private and family life and the right to marry and found a family. Those two rights stem from the second world war, when the Nazis banned sexual relations between people of different races. But Ms Deech sees people interpreting the new law as an absolute right to have a child regardless of sexual orientation or age.

For example?

Ms Deech says: 'If a single woman were rejected for treatment by a clinic she might say "I demand my human rights", if a lesbian couple, perhaps, had a baby abroad or were rejected by a clinic here, they would challenge any refusal to treat them like a heterosexual couple, because there is a clause which says the rights and liberties in this act must be extended to people without discrimination or status.'

What was a recent controversy involving the HFEA?

The HFEA opposed the decision by Diane Blood to have a child with her dead husband's sperm. But Ms Blood went to court and, after a four-year legal battle, gave birth to her son. Ms Deech remains convinced the HFEA's 21-strong committee made the right decision as 'you don't carry out medical procedures on the dying or unconscious'.

© Guardian Newspapers Limited, 2000

Fertility – introduction

Information from the Centre for Reproductive Medicine

About 1 in 6 of all couples seek specialist help because of difficulty in conceiving, though that includes some trying for a second pregnancy. That remarkable statistic should not be surprising if we appreciate that human fertility is relatively inefficient. The over-population of our world with people is because we have learned to be efficient survivors; we are relatively poor reproducers!

Amongst couples of *proven normal* fertility the highest conception rate *per monthly cycle* is 33% (1 in 3), occurring in the first month. The monthly rate then falls quickly, to about 5% (1 in 20). The normal average is only 20-25% (1 in 4 or 5). One in 10 fertile couples (10%) take more than one year to conceive, and 1 in 20 (5%) take more than 2 years, just by chance.

Fertility is a matter of chance. Like trying to throw a '6' with dice, you may be lucky first time, but there is no guarantee you will succeed even after lots of attempts. As with normal fertility, so it is with infertility treatments. Any treatment that offers as much as 25% chance of conception each cycle is as good as can be expected by reference to normal fertility statistics.

Therefore many couples who have been trying to conceive for only a year or two are normal, and will conceive without help. But of course some will have a real cause therefore *all* deserve to be investigated. The basic screening tests can be done by your GP. If they give no pointers to a specific cause it would be better not to proceed too quickly to specialist tests/investigations until after 1-2 years. Women over 35 years old, however, have no time to lose and would have a strong case to proceed quickly, after one year at most.

Outline of assisted conception treatments

IVF – In-vitro fertilisation

Fertilisation *in vitro* means, literally, fertilisation in glass. Eggs that have been stimulated to maturity are collected by needle from the ovaries. This is done using ultrasound screening or laparoscopy, according to individual needs.

The eggs are fertilised in the laboratory by the husband's sperms which are collected and specially prepared on the same day. After 2 or 3 days the fertilised eggs (now called embryos) are transferred to the womb (uterus) through the cervix. If pregnancy occurs it continues in the natural way.

IVF treatment was originally devised to bypass blocked or damaged tubes which prevent the passage of eggs to the uterus. But it has now proved valuable particularly in the treatment of prolonged unexplained infertility, endometriosis and sperm problems. It also offers the ultimate diagnostic test of fertilising ability of both eggs and sperm, which helps to encourage some couples to return to previously unsuccessful conventional treatments if still necessary.

In addition, women with a premature menopause can receive eggs collected from a donor and fertilised in the laboratory by their own husband's sperms. Shortage of suitable donors, however, makes it difficult to offer this treatment without delay.

ICSI – Intra-Cytoplasmic Sperm Injection

ICSI is a specialised laboratory technique for IVF. It involves all the same preliminary treatment and collection of eggs. When fertilisation has failed or is impossible because the sperm are severely defective or too few in number, fertilisation can be assisted by injecting the sperm directly into the eggs. A glass pipette (like a needle) which is several times finer than a human hair, is used to pick up a single sperm and pierce the covering layers of the egg to inject the sperm into the fluid contents of the egg cell (called its cytoplasm).

GIFT– Gamete Intra-Fallopian Transfer

When fertilisation proves normal and the tubes are healthy, other treatments can be used. GIFT involves all the same preparations as for IVF including egg recovery and sperm preparation. But at the same operation to collect the eggs they are mixed with the sperms (gamete means egg or sperm) and transferred immediately to the Fallopian tubes. That is where fertilisation occurs in the natural process.

IUI – Superovulation with Intra-Uterine Insemination

IUI involves similar preparations as for IVF and GIFT to stimulate multiple ovulation and prepare the sperms. But ovulation is allowed to occur without an operation to collect the eggs, and the sperms are injected high into the uterus to reach the eggs in the Fallopian tubes soon after the eggs have been released.

Other related treatments

There are several variations on the assisted conception treatments already described, which you may have heard about. They offer no special advantages but they may be necessary in rare circumstances because of particular technical problems.

The treatment methods

Information from the Centre for Reproductive Medicine

Apart from requiring technical ability to collect eggs, prepare sperms and handle and transfer embryos, the techniques adopted for preparing the way towards collecting the eggs are based on two essential requirements: the need to stimulate the production of several mature eggs, and the need to control the exact timing of ovulation (egg release from the ovarian follicles).

The chance of a single fertilised egg (or embryo) leading to pregnancy after transfer to the uterus is about 15%, varying mainly with age. Therefore, to make the intense effort worthwhile it is aimed to achieve 2-3 embryos for transfer, so increasing the chance of a pregnancy to over 30%. Of course that carries with it a small chance of 2 or all 3 embryos succeeding, therefore no more than 2-3 are transferred. This is a matter of ethical policy and regulatory constraint which will be discussed later.

On average, given healthy eggs and sperms, it requires 4-5 mature eggs to get 3 fertilised and developing as normal embryos. Powerful stimulation of the ovaries is therefore used (by injections like the natural gonadotrophin hormone, FSH), and the ovarian response needs to be monitored (a) to check that the response is sufficient and (b) to choose the right time to collect eggs.

There is usually little risk of the ovarian response being inadequate to proceed further, except in women over 40. The main risk is from premature ovulation, caused by the spontaneous occurrence of the natural trigger to ovulation, namely the LH (hormone) surge. The aim is to anticipate the LH surge by giving an injection of another hormone, HCG, which substitutes for it. That leads to the final stage of maturation of the eggs and to ovulation, which would occur after 38 hours. Egg collection can be timed shortly before that.

But the occurrence of a premature LH surge would foil that plan. It is not practically possible to detect the onset of the surge accurately and deal with it accordingly. Furthermore, the LH surge is often preceded by a gradual rise in LH levels (due to the stimulation) which can be harmful to the eggs. Therefore preliminary treatment is given to block the natural production of LH by the pituitary gland.

That treatment is by a synthetic preparation (e.g. buserelin) related to the natural releasing hormone for LH, and is available as a nasal spray which is more economic for brief use, or a monthly depot injection which is more convenient for prolonged use. This treatment is usually started about 2 weeks before the stimulation with FSH, and is continued until stimulation is completed after another 2 weeks when ready for egg collection. The controlling action of buserelin is further enhanced by an accompanying course of progestogen tablets for the first week.

IVF

Each cycle of treatment commences with a planning appointment with one of the IVF specialist nurses, to arrange a detailed calendar of events.

The progestogen tablets and buserelin treatments begin about one week before the menstrual period is due to start at the beginning of the actual IVF cycle. Buserelin is taken as a nasal spray every four hours except in the night.

After at least 14 days of buserelin, and following the menstrual period, stimulation with FSH begins, one injection daily. Seven days later there will be a visit to the clinic for the first monitoring by an ultrasound scan. That is mainly to check the ovarian response and for possible adjustment of the FSH dose. Depending on the ovarian response, there may be another one or more visits during the next week as the ovarian follicles approach readiness for egg collection.

The injections can be given at these clinic visits, but in between they could be given by your GP's nurse in his/her local surgery. However the newer preparations can be self-administered by automatic injection just under the skin, which is easy to do and much more convenient.

When the ovarian follicles are ready, arrangements will be made for the HCG injection to be given at a particular time late in the evening, and for egg collection 2 mornings later.

On the day of egg collection, the woman will be admitted to hospital that morning and return home in the afternoon or early evening. The man will need to produce his semen sample early the same morning for sperm preparation. Egg collection will be done by whichever method is most appropriate, usually ultrasound screening or occasionally laparoscopy (sometimes both), under intravenous sedation or general anaesthetic. Even when only intravenous sedation is used it will always be administered by a specialist anaesthetist to provide the best and safest service, and to be able to proceed to a general anaesthetic if necessary (although unlikely).

If fertilisation is successful, embryo transfer will be done 2 or 3 days after egg collection. It involves passing a fine tube through the cervix. It usually causes no more discomfort than the passing of the vaginal speculum, which has to stay in place a few minutes, and seldom any pain. It therefore requires no anaesthesia, and you can return home soon afterwards and to normal activity the next day. If any real difficulty is encountered we would arrange to try again the next day under general anaesthetic.

After the embryo transfer, all you can do is wait in hope. If pregnancy fails to occur menstruation will follow about 14 days after egg collection.

Should the treatment fail there will be a subsequent consultation to review the details and advise on future treatment as appropriate.

You might like to know that all the steps in the treatment cycle as described above are included in the charge, apart from the drugs.

Storage of extra embryos

If more than 2 or 3 embryos are achieved for transfer, the extra embryos will be frozen for storage if you wish, if they are suitable. They can then be transferred in a subsequent cycle without having to collect further eggs. There will be additional charges for those procedures.

We would only offer to store embryos which appear well enough developed to survive freezing and thawing. However, we cannot store any embryos from couples who are potentially infectious (e.g. with hepatitis virus) because of the risk of contamination of embryos from other couples which must share storage in the same liquid nitrogen container.

ICSI

The procedures are the same as for IVF, except that fertilisation is achieved by injecting a single sperm into each egg, as described earlier.

Assisted hatching

The early embryo is enclosed in a shell called the zona pellucida.

In order for the embryo to develop into a baby it must break through this shell in a process called hatching. We have a laser assisted hatching system for use in appropriate cases.

Assisted hatching does not improve the chances of pregnancy for everyone having IVF or ICSI, but recent work suggests that it may be helpful in the following circumstances:

* Women over 38 years having IVF or ICSI
* Frozen embryo replacement
* Following three unsuccesful IVF or ICSI cycles
* Patients with extra thick zona pellucida

GIFT

The procedures are the same as for IVF, as described above, except for the following:

1. Laparoscopy, including general anaesthesia, is always needed in order to transfer the eggs along with the prepared sperms into the Fallopian tubes.

2. There is no embryo transfer. The costs are the same because any saving on the embryo transfer is offset by the more complex procedure at egg recovery to transfer the eggs and sperms to the Fallopian tube by laparoscopy.

Superovulation and IUI

The basic principles of making several eggs available and delivering prepared sperms as close as possible to the eggs in the Fallopian tubes are similar to the aims of GIFT. But there are two important differences that affect the way the treatment is carried out in practice:

1. IUI is carried out only after ovulation has occurred (i.e. after the ovarian follicles have ruptured to release the eggs) and therefore does not need to be so carefully timed as egg collection for IVF or GIFT. Thus premature ovulation does not matter, and the simplest drug treatment can be used (clomiphene and FSH).

2. Because eggs are not collected artificially the only ways to limit the risk of multiple pregnancy is by using a low dose of FSH to restrict the number of follicles stimulated. That further reduces the drug costs. However, too many follicles can develop despite that precaution, in which case IUI treatment would need to be cancelled. The alternative would be to proceed to IVF or GIFT instead and to store any extra fertilised eggs.

Surgical sperm recovery

When there is an uncorrectable blockage to sperm, as can occur naturally or in some cases of vasectomy, sperm can be collected from behind the blockage by a minor surgical procedure. Sperm can usually also be collected from a small tissue sample taken directly from the testis in cases of severe lack of sperm production. Either way, the sperm are relatively few and immature but usually sufficient to achieve fertilisation by ICSI.

Sperm collection from men with spinal injuries by electroejaculation

Men with ejaculatory failure due to nerve damage caused by spinal injury, and occasionally by other conditions, can produce sperm by electrical stimulation of the ejacula-tory ducts internally. Though sperm quality is often poor due to remaining too long in the body, the sperm are usually suitable for ICSI treatment.

Treatment using donor sperm

If for any reason, sometimes genetic, a man's own sperm are unsuitable, a couple may choose treatment using donor sperm instead. In that case simple insemination would usually be the choice method of treatment, but there may be additional reasons why IVF might be needed using donor sperm.

Donor sperm treatment is readily available but involves important emotional, ethical and legal issues requiring special consideration and counselling. Those issues are covered in detail in a separate information booklet.

Treatment using donor eggs

Donor eggs are required by women who have a premature menopause, or by women who are still ovulating but whose egg quality and production are severely reduced by age.

Donor egg treatment involves IVF, using sperm from the recipient's husband to fertilise the donor eggs. The donor undergoes all the treatment to stimulate multiple ovulation and collect eggs, as described for IVF. The recipient woman undergoes simple hormonal treatment to prepare her uterus for implantation, and the embryos are transferred in the usual way.

Donor egg treatment is discussed in detail in a separate booklet, including the special emotional, ethical and legal issues involved.

Donor embryos

Rarely, a couple may need both donor eggs and donor sperm. An obvious answer would seem to be the many frozen embryos stored for other couples who had successful IVF treatment and no longer need the extra embryos. Unfortunately it is practically impossible to undertake the detailed health checks and counselling which would be required on every couple before their treatment. Therefore couples needing both donor eggs and donor sperm would in practice undergo donor egg treatment, as described above, combined with use of donor sperm.

Changes in treatment methods

Infertility medicine is advancing quickly, and the University of Bristol's Centre for Reproductive Medicine is at the forefront of clinical and laboratory research, not simply in technical develop-ments but in basic understanding of the causes of infertility. You as patients benefit directly from our scientific approach to the speciality, which includes not only innovation but careful evaluation of new techniques. The methods described above may therefore change in some respects by the time you come through for treatment and we may advise variations to suit specific needs of some couples.

One in five fertility treatments are a success

By Cherry Norton, Health Correspondent

Couples using fertility treatment to conceive have a 30 per cent greater chance of having a healthy baby than they did at the beginning of the decade, because of advances in test-tube baby treatments.

The latest figures, published today by the Human Fertilisation and Embryology Authority, show that, on average, one in five treatments conducted last year ended with the birth of a baby. At the beginning of the decade the national average was 14 per cent. It is estimated that one in seven couples has problems conceiving and increasing numbers are seeking fertility treatment. Last year more than 26,685 women underwent in-vitro fertilisation (IVF) treatments in clinics in Britain. These resulted in the birth of 4,138 single babies, 1,441 pairs of twins, and 176 sets of triplets.

More than a third of all women, 35 per cent, now only have two fertilised eggs implanted rather than three. Doctors used to prefer to implant more embryos to increase the chances of success but the greater risk of complications, as well as the enormous emotional and financial pressure on parents, has led to a reduction in the number used.

Advances in methods and the increasing numbers of women seeking treatments has led to the greater success of the treatment. One of the greatest advances was the introduction in 1993 of Intra-Cytoplasmic Sperm Injection.

After initial success rates of 3.8 per cent, this now has a success rate of 20.7 per cent, and is used in over a quarter of all IVF treatments. The technique is used to alleviate low sperm counts and involves a single sperm being injected directed into an egg.

The main factors that determine success are the age of the woman, the length of time the couple have been trying to have a family and the quality of the sperm. The woman's age is one of the strongest indicators of whether or not the treatment will be successful with women aged 45 and over having only a 5 per cent chance of having a baby using IVF.

A shortage in the number of donated eggs, required when a woman's own eggs are too old or not good enough, has led to a stagnation in the number of babies born using another woman's genetic material. Last year 355 babies were born using donated eggs or embryos compared with 329 in 1998. In Britain it is illegal to pay somebody for their eggs, although egg-sharing schemes in which a woman receives free fertility treatment if she donates some of her eggs are now available in some clinics. Many couples are forced to travel to America to acquire eggs at an average cost of $10,000 (£6,250).

The Patients' Guide to IVF Clinics shows for the first time success rates broken down by age. Some clinics, including St Mary's Hospital, Manchester, and University Hospital Aintree in Liverpool had no success with treating women over the age of 38 last year.

In-vitro fertilisation

Information from ISSUE

What is IVF?

In-vitro fertilisation, sometimes called test-tube fertilisation and often shortened to IVF, is a treatment that has helped several thousand couples achieve parenthood in the years since the first baby conceived after IVF was born in 1978.

IVF is the process of collecting oocytes (eggs) from a woman and fertilising them with spermatozoa outside the body. 'In-vitro' simply means in glass, and refers to the fact that all test tubes were once glass. Most IVF is in fact now done in plastic dishes called petri dishes.

When is IVF useful?

It should be stressed that IVF is not a suitable treatment for all infertility, about 20% of infertility cases may benefit from it. The eggs are fertilised outside the body, bypassing the Fallopian tubes; therefore IVF is an ideal treatment option for couples where the infertility is due to blockages of the Fallopian tubes. IVF can also be useful as a treatment for couples where the infertility is unexplained, caused by cervical mucus problems or endometriosis. It can also be an effective method of dealing with some male fertility problems.

What does IVF involve?

Background

Every month women develop several eggs from one of their ovaries, but usually only one is chosen by the body to be released into the Fallopian tubes. There are two methods of IVF, Stimulated Cycle IVF and Natural Cycle IVF. Most IVF units stimulate the ovaries to produce more than one egg, so that they have a greater chance of collecting at least one that is healthy. Natural Cycle IVF does not involve drugs, instead the one egg that develops naturally each month is collected.

Stimulated Cycle IVF

Several drugs can be used to stimulate egg production. Your IVF unit will choose the most suitable method for you when they have discussed your particular problem. There are three phases in the drug treatment:

1. LHRH analogue

A drug called an LHRH analogue is used to suppress the woman's own hormones and 'down regulate' her cycle. The LHRH analogues usually used by clinics in the UK are Buserelin or Nafarelin, which are usually taken as a nasal spray. These have the side effect of temporarily putting the woman who takes them through the menopause (the 'change') and she may experience symptoms such as hot flushes.

2. FSH or hMG

Whilst the LHRH analogue is being taken, a drug called Follicle Stimulating Hormone (FSH) or human Menopausal Gonadotrophin (hMG) is given. These drugs act on the ovary to make it produce more eggs than it would normally do. The drugs used in the UK for this purpose are Metrodin-HP, Humegon, or the latest recombinant drugs Gonal-F or Puregon by injection. They need to be given every day until the egg follicles on the ovary have grown sufficiently – usually about eleven days. Their effects need to be closely monitored and regular blood tests will be taken. Many women prefer to give their own injections, or ask their partners to give them; they find going to the IVF unit or going to see their own doctor every day stressful. It may be possible to seek out a local nurse who would be willing to give the injections in your own home; you could try asking nursing agencies.

3. Human Chorionic Gonadotrophin – hCG

After the last injection of FSH or hMG an injection of the hormone Human Chorionic Gonadotrophin (hCG) is given to mature the eggs. The eggs must be collected 34-36 hours later, otherwise there is the chance that ovulation could occur – i.e. the eggs could be released from the ovary – before they have been collected. Since most units collect them in the morning this means you need the injection late at night.

Do the drugs have side effects?

No drug is absolutely safe and completely free of side effects but with the doses of drugs used any side effects experienced are unlikely to be serious from a medical point of view. There is no evidence that fertility medicines cause ovarian cancer, but scientists are still studying that possibility. The doctors whom you see at the clinic will explain any side effects to you.

With all fertility drugs the biggest worry is that they may do their job too well and stimulate the ovary to produce too many eggs, a condition called Ovarian Hyper-stimulation Syndrome. Severe cases are rare, but it can cause some pain or discomfort in the abdomen. Close monitoring of the cycle ensures that this risk is kept to a minimum. If you experience severe abdominal pain or discomfort, seek medical advice.

Monitoring

Once you have started treatment, the IVF unit needs to find out how well your body is responding. There are many ways of doing this, and most use a combination of blood test and ultrasound scans, although some still rely on urine hormone measurements. Most IVF units use an ultrasound scanner that scans the ovaries and uterus via the vagina.

Egg retrieval

The eggs are collected from the ovaries, usually with a suction needle guided by ultrasound. It is usually an outpatient or day-care procedure. A needle is inserted into the ovaries via the vagina, guided by two ultrasound probes. The fluid from each follicle is aspirated into tubes and examined by an embryologist, who looks for eggs. Each portion of fluid is examined in turn and this is continued until every possible egg has been collected. Very rarely (in about 1% of cases), eggs are not found in the follicles.

The drugs used to ease the pain of egg recovery are mild sedatives, so for the next day or two you can feel fine but your reactions are slower. For the first 24 hours after egg recovery it is unsafe to drive, drink alcohol or use machinery. You may need to take time off work to recover and get over the fatigue of the treatment.

Embryology

After the eggs have been collected, the next stage is to put the best of the spermatozoa from the sperm sample with them. The spermatozoa are washed and prepared and put with the eggs, usually in the late afternoon. The day after egg collection the embryologist can often tell if fertilisation has happened by examining the eggs. Usually about 60-70% of eggs will fertilise, occasionally more, but not all eggs will fertilise normally. Most clinics look at the amount of cell division that has occurred and have a system of grading embryos, so that only the healthy ones are used.

Embryo transfer

Two days after the eggs have been removed and if they have fertilised and are developing normally, they are transferred to the womb. This procedure is quick and simple. A fine plastic tube containing the embryos is passed through the cervix (the neck of the womb), and the embryos put into the womb. Since most embryos do not develop into babies, most IVF units put more than one embryo into the womb. For younger women with good quality embryos, most clinics now prefer to put back only two. Since putting more than three embryos into the womb can result in high order multiple pregnancies, which are associated with an increased risk of pregnancy loss and decreased birth weight, the Human Fertilisation & Embryology Authority has ruled that no more than three embryos should be transferred. Good quality excess embryos can be frozen if the clinic has facilities for this – see later.

After transfer

The drugs that have been given may cause the ovaries to produce less of the hormone called progesterone than usual. Most IVF units therefore either give injections or pessaries of progesterone and/or HCG.

Success rates

The first thing to mention is that IVF does not work every time. In every unit in the world, IVF fails more often than it succeeds. It is also important to be aware that the treatment cycle can fail at any stage and may have to be abandoned – it may be that no eggs are produced or that too many are, or in some cases no eggs fertilise so there are no embryos to be transferred.

National pregnancy rates are published annually by the Human Fertilisation & Embryology Authority. Clinics vary in their success rates, but the differences cannot be assumed to be an indicator of the competence of different clinics. Some clinics are more willing than others are to treat older or more intractable fertility problems, which may lower their success rates.

The success rate of IVF treatment can vary between 15-25% per cycle but the likelihood of success declines as the woman gets older, particularly once she is over 35. For this reason it is important to ask the clinic about their success rates for women of a similar age to yourself.

Not every positive pregnancy test results in a baby. IVF pregnancies are more likely to result in miscarriage (about 20-25%) and also in ectopic pregnancy – which develops in the Fallopian tube (about 2-4%). This may be because IVF is not yet perfect or because women undergoing IVF are likely to be older and have more fertility problems than other women.

Natural Cycle IVF

Natural cycle IVF is where the woman receives no stimulation and the single egg produced naturally is collected, hopefully fertilised and then the resulting embryo transferred to the uterus.

The first IVF baby, Louise Brown, was a natural cycle birth, so it does work. The reason the medical profession went on to stimulation was because most embryos do not implant. Maybe 70% of the embryos in a three-embryo transfer still fail to produce a pregnancy.

Diagnosis

If there are some subtle hormone problems these can be studied in a natural cycle IVF and the levels of the woman's own hormones in a cycle can be carefully monitored. The main reason for doing the natural cycle in this case is to gain information about the patient and decide how best to treat them.

Treatment

A young woman with blocked tubes may not need the full stimulated cycle IVF. Some feel that they do not like the volume of drugs that are required in stimulated IVF, and of course natural cycle is cheaper.

'In-vitro' simply means in glass, and refers to the fact that all test tubes were once glass. Most IVF is in fact now done in plastic dishes called petri dishes

---

Success

Pregnancy success rate for natural cycle IVF are usually about half the rates of stimulated cycle, so a pregnancy rate per cycle of 10-15% would be a good rate for natural cycle IVF.

Cost

There are emotional and financial costs to IVF. There are few wholly NHS clinics and, even then, it is likely that you will have to pay some of the cost of treatment. Private health insurance generally has strict limitations on fertility treatment and it should not be assumed that the cost of your treatment will be covered. You will need to check your insurance policy.

Always get a clear estimate of the financial cost before you go for treatment. Services that appear cheap may charge extra for ultrasound scans and blood tests. Ask if there is an extra charge for freezing embryos not transferred.

Drugs costs can be significant, possibly adding in the region of 30% to the quoted cost of the treatment. Also dosages can alter substantially during the treatment cycle, which will affect the total drug cost. Your GP may prescribe some drugs on the NHS, which will help, but even NHS hospitals find it difficult to provide them.

The length of the treatment cycle can vary as can the timing of certain stages of treatment; for instance the day of egg collection may not be decided on until 48 hours or less beforehand. This can be quite stressful as regards taking time off work. You may have many visits to the clinic with some overnight stays necessary.

Freezing

Embryos not transferred can be frozen in liquid nitrogen, a process known as cryopreservation. Once frozen they could survive for centuries! Generally, pregnancy rates with frozen embryo transfer are not as good as they are with fresh embryos. They do however provide another attempt at becoming pregnant should the first one fail. You should be aware that not all embryos survive the freezing and thawing out process, but those that do may be replaced in monitored natural cycles or in hormone controlled cycles. Both partners' consent is needed to store embryos and you must also give your consent as to how they are used. You can use them yourself in a future treatment cycle as discussed, donate them to another couple, or donate them for research. This is entirely up to you and the clinic must have your consent before proceeding with any of these options. If the maximum storage period expires you need to consent to your embryos being stored for a longer period; if the clinic does not have your consent your embryos will be taken out of storage and allowed to perish. The maximum storage time now allowed by law is five years, extendable to ten years.

© ISSUE

New egg fusion technique

Information from Progress Educational Trust

A team of French, Spanish and Italian researchers has developed a new technique that may allow some infertile women to have their own genetic child. The new method, reported by the scientists in this month's issue of *Human Reproduction*, involves replacing the genetic information of a donor egg with that of the patient's egg.

The technique could help those women whose embryos repeatedly fail to develop because of problems with the egg cell cytoplasm, which surrounds the nucleus. Although this problem affects less than ten per cent of women attending fertility clinics, they can currently only be treated using donated eggs. But by transferring the nucleus of one of her eggs to a donor egg with its nucleus removed, such a woman may be able to have a child who is almost entirely genetically her own (with the exception of the 37 genes present in the cytoplasm).

The team has successfully managed to transfer egg nuclei to donor eggs using two approaches. One method involves using a chemical 'glue' called phytohaemagglutin, and the other involves a delicate microscopic manipulation similar to that used for intracytoplasmic sperm injection (ICSI). 'Because ICSI will probably be the best way of fertilising the reconstructed eggs the mechanical method we've developed will have the advantage of simultaneously fusing the eggs and introducing the sperm in a single, relatively simple action', said Dr Jan Tesarik, head of the team.

So far, the scientists have not attempted to fertilise any of the reconstructed eggs, because the formation of embryos for research purposes is banned in France and Spain and strictly regulated in Italy. But Dr Tesarik believes they are now ready to try and develop treatment for women who might benefit from the technique.

A spokesman for the UK's Human Fertilisation and Embryology Authority said that any UK clinic wishing to offer the technique could apply for a licence to create embryos using the method, but that doctors would have to satisfy the authority that the technique was safe before a licence could be granted. A spokesman for the fertility group Issue said the technique may assist thousands of couples to have their own baby.

• The above is an extract from *BioNews*, produced by the Progress Educational Trust.

© *Progress Educational Trust*

Surrogacy – fact and opinion

Information from LIFE

What surrogacy is

A surrogate mother bears a child for another man and woman and gives the child to the 'commissioning' couple soon after birth.

Who the 'commissioning' couple are

The law talks about 'husband and wife', a married couple who cannot bring a child of their own to birth. In practice, the commissioning couple do not need to be married or, indeed, to be male and female. It is possible for men and women in 'same sex' relationships to commission a surrogate to bear a child for them, either by using their own sperm or eggs, or by use of anonymous ('donor') sperm and egg.

How the baby is conceived

There are six possible ways:

- the surrogate mother has normal intercourse with the commissioning father.
- the baby is manufactured by IVF using the eggs and sperm of the commissioning couple, and the resulting embryos are placed in the surrogate for pregnancy to continue.
- the baby is manufactured by IVF using the egg of the commissioning mother and sperm from a, usually anonymous, donor.
- the baby is manufactured by IVF using the egg of a, usually anonymous, donor and the sperm of the commissioning father.
- the baby is manufactured from the sperm and egg of, usually anonymous, donors.

Who becomes a surrogate mother?

- women who are recruited by agencies which arrange introductions between commissioning couples and would-be surrogates. It seems that such agencies can be set up by anyone who so wishes.

The law relating to surrogacy is set out in the Surrogacy Arrangements Act 1985, which prohibits advertising by surrogacy agencies or by couples looking for a surrogate. So the recruitment is by word of mouth.

- mothers, sisters or other close female relatives of the commissioning couple.
- friends of the commissioning couple.

Payment of the surrogate mother

- the Surrogacy Arrangements Act forbids payment of surrogate mothers, but allows expenses to be paid. When the surrogacy arrangement is made through an agency there is payment by the commissioning couple of between £8,000 and £15,000. This payment is not described as a salary or fee, but 'expenses' and is presumably untaxed. The agent takes her own 'expenses'.
- when the surrogate is a relation or friend there is usually no financial reward.

Why anyone would want to be a surrogate mother

- some surrogate mothers do it for money.
- when the surrogate is a relation or close friend the motivation may be an altruistic wish to help the commissioning couple's childlessness.
- all surrogacy arrangements to a greater or lesser extent confer on the surrogate a sense of power over the commissioning couple.

Why that is so

Until the baby is handed over the surrogate mother is, in law, the mother of the baby even if the baby is not genetically her own child. She has the right to refuse to give the baby to the commissioning couple after birth. During the pregnancy she will usually be the object of deep concern of the commissioning couple for whom she is providing a much-wanted child. She has great power over them until she gives them the child.

What the law says

The Human Fertilisation and Embryology Act 1990 is the Act of Parliament that covers all artificial reproduction, including surrogacy. It amends the Surrogacy Arrangements Act 1985. The 1990 Act states that the commissioning couple (called husband and wife in the Act) must apply within 6 months of the birth to the surrogate mother of the child they have commissioned for a court order to enable that child to be treated in law as the child of the commissioning couple.

The 1990 Act states that both the father of the child, even if he is not genetically the father, and the surrogate mother have to agree to the court order with full understanding of what is involved.

The court has to be satisfied that no money or other benefit, other than for expenses reasonably incurred, has been given or received by the commissioning couple to ensure that the court order is made or to encourage the surrogate to hand over the child to the commissioning couple.

The 1990 Act does not overturn the 1985 Act's statement that 'no surrogacy arrangement is enforceable by or against any of the persons making it'.

If these rules are followed the laws on adoption do not apply to surrogacy. There is no legal requirement that the commissioning couple must be suitable and willing to bring up the child in an environment that is best for the child.

There is no regulation of the agencies that arrange surrogacy. There seems to be no interference by officials if and when the child is handed over to the surrogate.

What this means for the child

There is no protection for the child. The strict laws controlling adoption are intended to protect children from being bought and sold, and/or from being given to couples who are deemed unsuitable to be parents or unable to bring up a child in an environment or culture that will be of benefit to the child. Modern adoption practices ensure that, as far as possible, the child knows the truth about his/her natural parentage. There is a lengthy process during which the natural parent can change her mind and withdraw. In adoption the child's interests are paramount in law and practice.

In surrogacy the needs or wishes of the adults are paramount. The child becomes a product to be manufactured to satisfy an adult need and, usually, to make money for another adult.

Surrogacy arrangements are not legally binding. It is possible that neither the surrogate nor the commissioning couple will want the child, if the child is, for example, born disabled or the 'wrong' sex or colour. There have been several lawsuits where surrogate mothers have refused to give up the child to the commissioning couple.

There has been publicity of cases when neither the surrogate nor the commissioning couple wanted the child after birth. There have been cases where the child has been aborted.

If surrogacy is achieved by use of anonymous donor sperm and/or eggs the child will not know who his/her genetic parents are.

There may well be deceit practised by the adults involved to deny the child knowledge of the circumstances of birth or parentage.

It is possible for a child to have 5 'parents' if conception is by IVF from donated egg and sperm: the two donors, the surrogate mother and the commissioning couple. If the child knows this he/she could be a very confused person. If the child is kept in the dark sooner or later the truth will out, and will hurt.

Drawbacks for the surrogate mother

- The surrogate mother bonds with

the baby during pregnancy, as in all pregnancies, especially if the child has been conceived naturally by her and is not an IVF product. The strong emotions after birth make it hard for the surrogate to part with the child, however 'businesslike' she may have been about conception and pregnancy. There have been several cases when the surrogate mother has not handed over the child.

- The surrogate mother usually has born children who will ask questions and feel strange emotions when they watch their mother give away the baby they've seen grow during pregnancy.

- The surrogate's husband or partner may have ambivalent feelings about the pregnancy and the effect on family life, even when there are sizeable 'expenses' as an inducement.

- If the pregnancy is achieved by IVF the surrogate's body has to be artificially prepared to be able

---

The other children of the surrogate mother must have very mixed feelings about their mother's behaviour

---

to carry the pregnancy. This under-reported problem affecting all IVF pregnancies involves injecting the surrogate with hormones to stimulate the natural process when the womb is prepared for implantation of the embryo. These drugs have long-term effects that are linked with cancer.

- If the commissioning couple pull out of the deal before birth the surrogate has to decide whether to keep the child or arrange adoption. In one case the commissioning couple told the surrogate to have an abortion when pre-birth screening tests showed the child had Down's Syndrome. The surrogate mother did not want an abortion. But neither did she want to have a disabled child. So she had an abortion that she afterwards regretted.

- If the surrogate is a friend or relation of the commissioning couple, there will be natural maternal feelings and sense of 'ownership' by the surrogate that could adversely affect her when the commissioning couple claim 'their' baby, and during the child's upbringing.

Is surrogacy ever right?

No one truly benefits from surrogacy. The child is created to satisfy a number of complicated adult desires with no protection from the law for the child if the deal goes wrong. Children should not be made to fulfil adult dreams and desires, whether by surrogacy or in the normal way. Children are a gift, not a commodity. Adults have no 'right' to have a child.

The child may grow up thinking that the commissioning couple are his/her genetic parents only to find out that they are not. There may be identity problems for the child, feelings of 'who am I?', 'where do I come from?'

The commissioning couple may satisfy their desire to have a child but at a possible cost to their own relationship. Whether they tell the child or not about the surrogacy arrangements, the child will soon find out and may well have problems with this knowledge that rebounds on the parents. If the child is conceived by donor eggs and/or sperm there could be complicated feelings in the person of the commissioning couple who is not the 'real' father or mother, which rebound on the couple's relationship. And what happens if neither is the genetic parent and the child has

---

More emphasis should be put on helping childless couples to adopt or foster children

---

problems, and one or other of the couple cannot cope or blames the unknown genetic parents?

The problems for the surrogate mother and her family seem obvious. In carrying the child to birth she forms a unique bond, whether or not the child is 'hers'. When she hands over the child she will suffer, especially as everyone who knows that she is pregnant also knows why and how she is pregnant. It's not like adoption – the mother does not deliberately enter into a formal arrangement in order to become pregnant. When the baby is born she goes for adoption because in that case it is best for the child.

The other children of the surrogate mother must have very mixed feelings about their mother's

behaviour. As young as two years old a child will take an interest in the baby growing inside his/her mother and be prepared to welcome the newcomer. The older the child the deeper the interest. What will a child feel if the mother returns from hospital without the baby, or gives the baby away during the 6 months after birth? What a role model for him/her.

As for the surrogate's male partner/husband, if there is one, what can he feel at this intrusion into his family life and what will other people think of him? And what a role model he is for his children.

What society should do

Surrogacy should be banned and surrogacy agencies outlawed. More emphasis should be put on helping childless couples to adopt or foster children and on counselling couples who cannot have children so that they come to accept that they can nonetheless lead rich, generous lives – and make a very worthwhile contribution to the world precisely because they do not have family responsibilities.

© *LIFE*

Surrogacy

Information from ISSUE

What is surrogacy?

A surrogacy arrangement is one in which one women (the surrogate mother) agrees to bear a child for another women or a couple (the intended parents) and surrender it at birth (HFEA & BMA *Considering surrogacy?* 1996).

However, although the defining characteristic of surrogacy is simple enough, surrogacy has many forms, some of which stem from the introduction of the new technologies and treatments such as IVF.

There is an important distinction between surrogacy where the surrogate mother contributes her own genes, and where she does not. Therefore, in any one type of surrogacy, the surrogate mother receives an embryo to bear and carry

to term though she contributes none of her own genes. This form of surrogacy the BMA terms 'full surrogacy', or we can think of it as 'host mothering' proper. In this situation, it is possible that the intended parents contribute the egg and the sperm and are the genetic parents. The other type of surrogacy, is where the surrogate mother is

---

Although the defining characteristic of surrogacy is simple enough, surrogacy has many forms

---

inseminated and therefore contributes her own egg. The BMA term this type of surrogacy 'partial surrogacy' and the surrogate mother is both the genetic and the carrying mother. In each type of surrogacy, however, the surrogate mother is defined as the legal mother since this status is always given to the carrying mother.

Surrogacy is further complicated. It may be initated via sexual intercourse or through artificial insemination. The surrogate mother may give her services free of charge, or claim for expenses. If anything more than expenses is paid that is against the Human Fertilisation and Embryology Act. The surrogate mother may be unknown to the couple, or could be a friend or close relative of the couple. If she is unknown, she could remain anonymous to the couple or the couple could come to know her and share certain aspects of the pregnancy. Each of these variations is possible and each has different implications for the people involved, all of which will need to be considered seriously. This article can only address some of these.

For whom is surrogacy appropriate?

As far as infertility is concerned surrogacy is of particular relevance for women who have difficulties in sustaining a pregnancy for whatever reason. By and large it will only be worth considering if all other reasonable means of trying to have a child have failed (or would obviously not be possible), and indeed, only if this is so is there likely to be medical help available.

Surrogacy and the law

There have been two recent pieces of legislation concerning surrogacy, namely the Surrogacy Arrangements Act 1985, and the Human Fertilisation and Embryology Act 1990. Together these acts make the position regarding surrogacy clear, but they do contain a lot of detail, and unfortunately, anyone contemplating surrogacy will need to understand how these details apply to them. ISSUE will be able to help.

The main point, however, is that surrogacy is not illegal. On the other hand, it can only be carried out under certain conditions and considerations and has far-reaching implications. The most important of these are as follows:

Surrogacy and commercialism

The acts prohibit any third party from acting on a commercial basis to help effect a surrogacy arrangement in any way. The Act also bans advertising – in any form or by anyone, whether a third party, the surrogate mother or the intended parents. The definition of what constitutes advertisement is very stringent: putting up a notice on a board could count! However, surrogacy itself is not illegal, and payments between the intended parents and the surrogate mother may be made provided there is no third party involved, and that they only cover expenses.

Surrogacy and legal parentage

It is the carrying mother, or the surrogate mother who is defined as the legal mother and who has prior rights to the child. This means that, whatever any initial contacts or arrangements, if the surrogate changes her mind and wishes to keep the child, she is at liberty to do so. Surrogacy contacts are therefore unenforceable. If the surrogate mother is married and her husband has agreed to the insemination, it is he who is defined as the legal father. Indeed, the only way parentage can be changed from the surrogate mother to the intended parents is via formal legal proceedings.

There is very little intending parents can do to secure their position prior to the birth particularly as the law does not recognise surrogacy as a binding agreement on the surrogate mother. However, from the point of birth onwards, it is possible for the biological father to enter into a Parental Responsibility Agreement with the surrogate mother. This places the father on an equal footing with the surrogate mother regarding their rights, duties and responsibilities to the child.

Until recently the only way intended parents could secure permanent and exclusive parental responsibility, in other words, full parenthood, of the child, was to apply for an adoption order. This is a long-winded procedure that involves several visits by a social worker as well as the involvement of a Guardian-ad-Litem who is appointed by the court on behalf of the child.

Since 1 November 1994 a procedure which seems in some ways to recognise for the first time the position of the intended parents in surrogacy is available. Section 30 of the Human Fertilisation & Embryology Act 1990 provides that a couple whose gametes (eggs and/or sperm) have been used in a surrogacy arrangement can apply for a Parental Order. This is a permanent order and it gives the couple full parental rights in exactly the same way that an Adoption Order would. However, it should be a much simpler and quicker procedure.

To qualify, the child must be living with the intended parents and they have to be married, over 18 and living in the United Kingdom, Channel Islands or Isle of Man. The intended parents must apply within six months of the birth of the child.

The intended parents will need to obtain Parental Order forms from their local Magistrate's Court. That

is the one where they and their child live rather than where the surrogate lives if they differ. The form tells them what to do and the court staff should be able to help them with any queries.

Disclosure of the surrogate mother's identity

Children whose intended parents have obtained a court order, will have the right to know the identity of the surrogate mother once they reach the age of 18.

Surrogacy and risk

Therefore, although surrogacy is not illegal, and couples can pay surrogate mothers directly, but only for expenses, intended parents face a good deal of risk and must realise at the outset that any contact they may set up with the surrogate mother will have no legal basis. The outcome of the Parental Order procedures described above cannot be guaranteed in advance. And they may well be made more difficult if any money has changed hands during the surrogacy, even if that money covered obvious expenses incurred by the surrogate mother. On the other hand, should the intended parents change their minds about having the child, it would be the surrogate mother who would have to retain parental rights and responsibilities – unless relieved of them by the social services. A further warning is that, if the surrogate mother was not married and wished to retain the child, if she has conceived via the semen of the intended father, he might be liable for maintenance payments for the child, although he would also have parental rights over the child.

Finally, on the question of risk, the intended parents should take out a life insurance policy to benefit the surrogate's family because of the hazards of pregnancy and childbirth faced by the surrogate mother. Also you should make/amend your Will in case anything should happen to you whilst the surrogate is pregnant.

Ethical implications

Legal consideration aside, surrogacy is controversial because it raises many sensitive ethical issues. Most of these can be resolved in relatively straightforward ways. However anyone seriously considering surrogacy would do well to discuss the ethical aspects with someone with knowledge and/or experience of surrogacy such as a representative of a voluntary organisation, a counsellor and if appropriate, a representative of their religious faith.

Surrogacy as 'unnatural'

Surrogacy is sometimes criticised because it is alleged to be 'unnatural': yet many infertility treatments are 'unnatural' in that they involve artificial means of conception and 'high tech' medical treatment. So this cannot be an argument against surrogacy, unless one also argues against techniques such as in-vitro fertilisation for example.

Surrogacy as 'undermining the family'

Others argue that surrogacy undermines the family. This argument is also difficult to sustain, because families in Britian are many and varied; indeed the ideal-typical nuclear family of a bread-winner father, married to a home-maker mother living together with their natural offspring make up less than 15% of all households in Britain. Further, while no one should underestimate the problems that surrogacy raises, there is no reason to believe that the difficulties are necessarily greater than for some other types of families which we accept.

Surrogacy and 'deceit'

Other arguments centre on the view that the parents who are bringing up a child may deceive it about its origins. Of course, during the years of infancy and childhood, the parents bringing the child up could mislead the child about how it was born. But it is questionable whether surrogacy should be prohibited because some may find it difficult to tell the child about its origins. And most will accept that it will be very difficult to sustain the secrecy, not least because as things stand, they will have had to take out a court order so that, once 18, the child will have the right to know the identity of his or her surrogate mother. Openness is desirable should there be any risk of an inherited genetic abnormality for the child to contend with. In most cases, therefore, surrogacy is likely to be open.

Surrogacy as 'selling babies'

Some of the strongest arguments about surrogacy concern the commercial aspects and that for example, 'selling' a baby degrades it. But, the involvement of third parties to arrange surrogacy on a commercial basis is illegal in Britain. Further, even where money changes hands between the intended parents and the surrogate mother, this can only be within the Human Fertilisation and Embryology Act if these only cover expenses. The Act prohibits the surrogate mother benefiting financially from her surrogacy. Furthermore, in some cases, the intended parents will be the genetic parents, while in many others the husband in that couple will be the genetic father. Even so, this is a particularly sensitive area and would need very careful handling with the growing surrogate child. Since surrogacy would be very difficult to keep secret, and the child would probably have the right to know its genetic parents at the age of 18 in any case, the best approach is probably one of honesty, openness and parental love to reassure the child that s/he was never just a commodity. And, as with so many children born of assisted reproduction, that child would be very much a wanted and planned addition to the family.

Surrogacy as 'exploitation of the surrogate mother'

Other arguments focus on the surrogate mother and point out, for example, that surrogacy could result in surrogate mothers becoming exploited. This argument too requires very serious attention. However, provided that a surrogacy arrangement was entered into freely by all parties, and the surrogate mother treated sensitively and with respect, exploitation is not something that need necessarily emerge. But it is a danger that must be guarded against and to which we must remain alert.
© ISSUE

Considering surrogacy?

Your questions answered

What is the legal position?

Surrogacy is not prohibited by the law. However, it is illegal for an individual or agency to act on a commercial (i.e. profit-making) basis to organise or facilitate a surrogacy arrangement for another person. Agencies or individuals may perform this function on a non-commercial basis and individual surrogate mothers may be paid expenses by the intended parents. All advertising that a person is willing to be a surrogate mother or that someone is looking for a surrogate mother is prohibited.

The law states that any clinic providing treatment involving the donation of eggs or sperm, or the creation of embryos outside the body, must be licensed by the regulatory body, the Human Fertilisation and Embryology Authority (HFEA). Full surrogacy, which involves the creation of embryos outside the body must therefore only be performed in a licensed clinic. Where the insemination with the intended father's sperm, in partial surrogacy, is performed by a health professional (thus using donated sperm), the premises on which the procedure takes place must also be licensed by the HFEA.

Are surrogacy arrangements legally enforceable?

No. Surrogacy arrangements are unenforceable in law. Therefore, irrespective of whether a contract has been signed, and whether any money has changed hands, either party could change its mind at any time. For this reason, it is particularly important that all parties have considered very carefully the implications of their decision to take part in a surrogacy arrangement. If any of the parties have any doubts about their commitment to the arrangement, they should say so before a pregnancy is established and the arrangement should not proceed.

What is the legal status of the child?

In law, the legal mother is always the carrying mother (i.e. the surrogate mother in a surrogacy arrangement). The legal father is rather more complicated. If the surrogate mother has a partner he will be the legal father of the child, unless he can show that he did not consent to the treatment. If the surrogate mother does not have a partner and the treatment did not take place in a licensed clinic (i.e. it was self-insemination), the intended father will be the legal father. If treatment was undertaken in a licensed clinic and the surrogate mother has no partner, the child will be legally fatherless. This has a number of implications. In order for the intended parents to become the legal parents of the child, they must either apply to adopt the child or apply for a parental order (see below). This is true even if they are the genetic parents of the child (i.e. their sperm and eggs were used). If the intended parents change their minds about taking the child, for example, if their circumstances have changed or if the child is born physically or mentally disabled and they feel unable to cope, the surrogate mother and her partner, if she has one, will be legally responsible for the child.

What is a parental order and who can apply for one?

A parental order, which is obtainable by application to the courts, makes the intended parents the child's legal parents. This has the same effect as adoption, but allows a quicker route in cases of surrogacy. In order to apply for a parental order, the following criteria must be met:

- the child must be genetically related to one or both of the intended parents;
- the intended parents must be married to each other and must both be aged 18 or over;
- the legal mother and father (i.e. the surrogate mother and her partner, if she has one) must consent to the making of the order (this consent cannot be given until six weeks after he birth of the child);

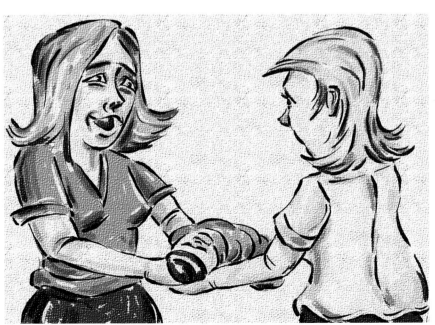

- no money other than reasonable expenses has been paid for the surrogacy arrangement unless the payment has been authorised by a court;
- the child must be living with the intended parents and one or both of the intended parents must be living in the UK;
- an application must be made within six months of the birth of the child.

A child born to a surrogate mother will be registered as her child and that of the legal father (see above). Where a parental order has been granted a separate entry will be made in a Parental Orders Register. However, it is not possible to abolish the original birth registration and at the age of 18, the child will be able to obtain a certified copy of the original record which will include the name of the surrogate mother. Prior to being given access to this information the person will be advised of the availability of counselling.

What are the criteria for becoming a surrogate mother?

A potential surrogate mother must be in good overall health and be able to undergo a pregnancy with the minimum amount of risk to her own health. Some medical conditions will prevent a woman becoming a surrogate mother, for example, if there are any known medical problems which could lead to complications with the pregnancy, or put the woman at risk. Also those who are considerably overweight, are heavy smokers, drinkers or substance abusers are not suitable as surrogate mothers because of the associated risks both to the woman and the baby. As the risks of illness and problems are much higher in the first pregnancy it is strongly recommended that surrogate mothers should have borne at least one child previously and preferably have completed her own family. This also means that the woman is able to give her 'informed' consent to the arrangement, since a woman who has experienced pregnancy prior to the surrogacy arrangement has that knowledge on which to base her decision. Only in very exceptional cases should a woman who has not

had a child herself consider becoming a surrogate mother. Because of the increased risk of chromosome abnormalities (e.g. Down's Syndrome) resulting from the eggs of an older woman, an upper age limit of 35 years is set for those donating eggs to other women. The same age should therefore apply to surrogate mothers whose own eggs are to be used, and because the risks of pregnancy increase with age, any woman over 35 should give careful consideration before deciding to become a surrogate mother.

Being a surrogate mother is an emotionally and physically demanding task. It is important that a woman considering this option has the backing of a partner, family or friends to provide emotional support and practical help throughout and after the pregnancy. Surrogacy is not something to enter into lightly. Careful consideration must be given to the medical, emotional, legal and practical issues, and to the implications of surrendering the child at birth. Thought must also be given to the effect on any existing children, the potential surrogate mother's partner, family and friends.

What are the health risks to the surrogate mother?

There is a risk of transmitting infection, such as HIV or hepatitis, to the surrogate mother from the intended parents. This risk can be reduced by testing and, if the sperm or embryos are quarantined, the risk is very small.

In full surrogacy, when more than one embryo is replaced into the surrogate mother's uterus, the risk of multiple pregnancy increases.

Around 20-25% of the pregnancies resulting from in-vitro fertilisation will result in a multiple pregnancy of twins or triplets, depending on the number of embryos replaced. This carries associated risks for both mother and babies and there are serious implications for the intended parents of raising children from a multiple pregnancy. In view of this high risk of multiple pregnancy, careful consideration should be given to the number of embryos to be replaced.

Surrogacy pregnancies are no more likely to have adverse effects on the woman's physical health than any other pregnancy (apart from risks associated with multiple pregnancy). However, it is important that before proceeding, the surrogate mother is aware of the usual risks of pregnancy. In very rare cases pregnancy can result in maternal death but more frequently less dramatic problems can arise during the pregnancy or in the period after the birth such as: gestational diabetes, high blood pressure, urinary-tract infections, haemorrhage, stress incontinence, painful intercourse and haemorrhoids. It is advisable for the intended parents to purchase insurance to cover the surrogate mother and her family in the event of any misfortune.

There is also a risk that the surrogate mother may suffer from post-natal depression. In addition to the usual factors accounting for post-natal depression, the surrogate mother may also feel a great sense of loss and bereavement at being separated from the baby she has carried for nine months.

Who should make decisions during and after the pregnancy?

Once an arrangement has been made, and before the pregnancy is established, a number of decisions need to be made about how the pregnancy should proceed. Ideally, a joint decision should be reached between the surrogate mother and the intended parents, although there may be times when their views will conflict. It is important that the issues are discussed before the surrogacy arrangement proceeds and it should be clear to everyone involved that the surrogate mother, with the advice of health professionals where appropriate, will make the final decisions during and immediately after the pregnancy.

The type of decisions which need to be made during the pregnancy might include the various tests to be undertaken such as ultrasound or blood tests and tests such as amniocentesis or Chorion Villus Sampling (CVS) to detect chromosome abnormalities. Consideration must also be given, in advance, as to how to proceed if a severe abnormality is detected. If, for example, the intended parents feel they would be unable to look after a child with a severe disability and the surrogate mother is opposed to termination, the parties need to decide how the situation would be managed and, if agreement cannot be reached, the surrogacy arrangement should not proceed. Cases may occur where one party has a change of mind when the situation arises but discussing the matter in advance should minimise the likelihood of this happening.

Decisions will also need to be made about the preferred method of delivery. It is important for all concerned to know if, for example, the surrogate mother wishes to give birth in water or if the intended parents are totally opposed to the use of drugs during delivery. Again, discussion should take place in advance of the pregnancy but final decisions about delivery should be made by the surrogate mother, with the advice of health professionals. Other decisions need to be taken immediately after the delivery about which parents would normally be consulted, such as in the case of a premature birth. Ideally, a joint decision should be reached but the surrogate mother has the right to make decisions about the child immediately after delivery. In the days after the delivery, provided the child has been passed to the intended parents, responsibilities for decision-making should pass to them.

Will the surrogate mother have contact with the intended parents and the child?
This will depend upon the individual circumstances and the

wishes of the parties concerned. It is important that this is discussed from the beginning so that problems do not develop at a later stage when the different expectations of the parties become apparent. Some surrogate mothers find it helpful to have the support of the intended parents throughout the pregnancy and equally the intended parents often want to share the experience and be involved with the pregnancy such as attending hospital for scans and possibly being present at, or immediately after, the birth. Others prefer to have limited contact.

Once the child is born the level of contact will again depend upon the wishes of the individuals concerned. In some cases, contact stops, by mutual agreement, as soon as the child is handed to the intended parents, except for the communication required for transferring the legal parentage of the child. In other cases the intended parents will send photographs of the child to the surrogate mothers and in some cases, the child will know the surrogate mother and her own family. What is important is that the surrogate mother and intended parents agree on a level of contact which they feel is appropriate for them.

What are the implications for the child?
One question which all intended parents have to deal with is whether to tell the child of his or her origins. Research shows that most people who have children conceived by surrogacy decide to explain the circumstances of their conception and birth to the child. If parents decide not to tell, they face a number of difficulties.

The number of children born as a result of surrogacy arrangements is small and there is a very limited amount of research available into the effects on the child

---

Surrogacy is difficult to conceal from others, and if other people know about the arrangement, there is the risk that the child may find out from them. The experience of learning in this way, and the discovery of deception by his or her parents, may be very distressing for a child. Another factor to be considered is that at the age of eighteen the child will have the legal right to discover the identity of his or her surrogate mother.

The number of children born as a result of surrogacy arrangements is small and there is a very limited amount of research available into the effects on the child. However, it has been suggested that such children may feel a certain amount of anxiety about being 'different' from their friends and may sometimes feel pressure to live up to the expectations of their parents who went to such great lengths to have them. However, these concerns do not appear to reflect the reality for children from other 'different' families, such as those resulting from infertility treatment or adoption. More positively it has been suggested that children conceived via surrogacy arrangements may in fact be proud of their parents' courage and grateful to their parents, and the surrogate mother, for their existence.

What happens now?
Surrogacy might be the only opportunity for some people to have children but it is not something which anyone should enter into lightly. Before deciding to enter into a surrogacy arrangement, either as a surrogate mother or an intended parent, it is important that the information contained in this article has been carefully considered and understood. It is a good idea to obtain as much information as possible, take time to reflect on it and, if possible, discuss it with partners, family or friends. Anyone with doubts about their commitment to surrogacy should not proceed any further.

• The above information is from the British Medical Association. See page 41 for address details.
© *British Medical Association (BMA)*

CHAPTER THREE: THE ETHICS

Family values and fertility issues

Information from the British Humanist Association

What is a family?

Families differ a great deal, from the traditional but relatively uncommon marriages where the father works and mother looks after the home and their 2.2 children, to families with one parent, families with many parents and step-parents, or parents of the same sex, and households with no children who consider themselves family. Some parents choose to remain unmarried, and some get married several times. Some children live with their natural parents, some are adopted or fostered, some are the results of IVF. Some families are large with supportive networks of aunts and uncles and grandparents; others are smaller or not so close. Add to this the fact that families belong to a range of communities and social, ethnic, religious and cultural groups, and there is bound to be considerable diversity in family life, something that humanists tend to welcome.

What are families for?

Human beings are essentially social animals, and we are very dependent on each other. Once we would have been totally dependent on people close to us, our family or tribe, for food shelter, protection, help with raising children and for company. The growing complexity of human society has meant that we are increasingly dependent on anonymous and distant people for many or our basic needs, and we have delegated many of the tasks that would originally have been done by the family. Supermarkets provide us with food, contractors build our houses, the state protects us, schools share the upbringing of our children, and so on. But much child care and many of our closest relationships are still found within the family, however one defines it. Families exist for mutual support, companionship, and the welfare of children.

Children are a serious commitment, and everyone wanting children should consider their situation carefully. Can they offer a child long-term support and stability? Can they give a children enough love and attention? Can they afford a child? Humanists believe that people should think about the consequences of their actions and make responsible and considered choices, taking the potential happiness of everyone involved into account.

What are family values?

'Family values' is a phrase often used by politicians to invoke a very traditional and unrealistic version of the family, and to try to impose restrictive and conventional standards of behaviour on people. 'Conventional' and 'traditional' values, though they may be good, are not *necessarily* good. Humanists believe that people should think for themselves and not risk making themselves and other people unhappy by being dogmatic about human relationships.

Family planning and fertility

Given these values and attitudes, it is not surprising that humanists have always been strong advocates of birth control. Indeed, an early humanist and founder of the National Secular Society, Charles Bradlaugh, was sentenced to six months in prison in 1877 for publishing a pamphlet about family planning with his friend Annie Besant. Unlike some opponents of birth control, humanists do not believe that contraception is wrong because it 'interferes with nature'.

Humanists do not believe that interfering with nature is in itself a bad thing, particularly if the consequences are good. Human beings interfere with nature all the time, for example, by wearing clothes or taking aspirin for headaches. If contraception results in every child being a wanted child, and in better, healthier lives for women, it must be a good thing. Humanists think that it would be unreasonable to condemn any arrangement which does no harm. When confronted with, for example, IVF, one should weigh up the consequences for those involved before judging, regardless of whether one would like the arrangements for oneself.

'Do as you would be done by' usually has to be tempered with a little empathy: seeing life from someone else's viewpoint and social context can be difficult, but it can prevent you from imagining that your personal preferences are absolute moral values to be imposed on everyone else.

One tradition which humanists would condemn because of its bad consequences is the tendency of some cultures to prefer children of one sex (usually male) to the other. This can lead to abortions because foetuses are the 'wrong' sex, or to infanticide or gross neglect of girl babies. IVF and other fertility treatments may make it easier to choose the sex of a child.

Ultimately, this can lead to a numerical imbalance between the sexes, as in China, with unfortunate consequences for family life – many heterosexual young men will never be able to find a wife to create their own families. Given the work that women do and the fact that both sexes are equally necessary for procreation, it is irrational to undervalue them, and it must cause a great deal of unhappiness as well as contravening the fundamental principle that we should treat everyone with equal respect.

From the topics covered above, you will have gathered that humanists have an open-minded and tolerant attitude to most family issues. They tend to judge individual situations compassionately, looking at short-and long-term consequences for the individuals involved and for society. New issues and ideas arrive all the time, and humanists are not limited in their thinking by traditional rules, sacred texts or authority figures. A few brief examples of new issues and the way in which humanists might think about them follow:

Gay marriage and parenthood were not issues in the public arena when homosexuality was illegal or taboo, and alternative methods of conception unavailable. Humanists oppose prejudice because it is unjust to discriminate against or punish people for aspects of themselves that are not matters of choice, such as race or sexuality Although the reasons for our own sexual preferences are not fully known, it seems unlikely that homosexuals could be 'cured' (as some Christian groups believe) any more than heterosexuals could be. (Some people may choose to be celibate but this should be a matter of choice, not compulsion.)

The question of whether gay couples should have children, by adoption or assisted conception, should surely be a question about their ability to be good parents. Usually people who really want children and are genuinely committed to having a family, are good(ish) parents – few people, even conventional heterosexual couples, are perfect parents! The difficulties that the children from unconventional families face are often social – teasing at school, lack of acceptance by neighbours or other family members – but may also be psychological – not knowing who one's father is, or lacking a role model for both sexes within the family unit. These problems do not only apply to the children of gay parents, and some are surmountable. Some would be overcome if society in general were more open-minded and tolerant of difference.

Assisted conception: IVF, fertility drugs, sperm donation, surrogate donation, surrogate pregnancies.

Human beings have long intervened in reproductive processes, usually to avoid unwanted pregnancies. We are increasingly able to intervene to help people have children, and this raises new ethical issues. Sometimes the method itself is problematical.

Surrogacy involves a third person, the surrogate mother, for nine months of the pregnancy. It is understandable that she would need compensation, but would a large reward encourage unconsidered involvement? Surrogates sometimes find it hard to relinquish the baby after birth, and deciding who is the child's real mother, who has a right to the child, and what and when to tell the child, are challenging problems.

Sperm donation can raise similar questions about a child's real father and also could, in theory, if not properly regulated, result in large numbers of half-siblings in the population.

Fertility drugs often result in multiple pregnancies and this can cause problems. Can the parents be good parents to so many babies all at once? Should multiple pregnancies where some or all of the foetuses will be damaged be allowed to continue? Should the extra foetuses be aborted and at what point? And what should happen to the spare embryos left after IVF?

Artificially increasing fertility raises other more general issues. Should the needs of potential children outweigh the desires of potential parents? Should middle-aged women be helped to have children when they can no longer conceive naturally? Should we deny people the chance to be parents when we know how to help them? Should society assist women to have children on their own, or help only wealthy women who will not be dependent on the state? Should we be increasing fertility when the world is already over-populated? Do artificial methods of conception increase population size (if they allow people to delay starting families, they might actually have the opposite effect)?

As you can see, difficult questions associated with human rights, individual happiness, scientific and medical progress, and social justice are at the heart of some of these issues.

Some further questions to consider

- Does everyone who wants a child have the right to have a child? Even if they cannot conceive naturally and need assistance from the National Health Service? Even if they cannot afford a child and will need financial support from the state in order to do so?
- Should religious people impose the moral and social edicts of their religion on non-religious people? Yes? Sometimes? Never?
- Can any activity which does not adversely affect anyone else be morally wrong?
  - Do humanist principles inevitably lead to liberal ideas about family values?
- How are you deciding your answers to these questions?

Taken from BHA briefing *Family Values*, Marilyn Mason, Education Officer.
© *British Humanist Association*

Infertility

Information from the Christian Medical Fellowship (CMF)

The Christian Medical Fellowship is a network of over 5,000 Christian doctors and medical students throughout the UK and Ireland who believe in God as revealed in the person of Jesus Christ, and who regard the Bible as the supreme authority in matters of faith and conduct. One of our official aims is to increase, in the medical profession, personal faith in Christ and acceptance of His ethical teaching, so we are interested in any issues at the interface of medicine and Christianity – infertility is certainly one such issue.

Most doctors define infertility as an inability to conceive after one year of trying, or an inability to carry pregnancies to a live birth. At least one in ten couples experience infertility and so it is a common problem.

Over the past 30 years there have been great advances in treatment for infertility. Medical treatment leads to successful pregnancies for over 50% of infertile couples and it is likely that this figure will rise further with the introduction of new methods of therapy. However, treatment does involve tests of both the male and female which are expensive and usually take many months to complete. Accordingly, the waiting, investigations and treatment can give rise to emotional distress.

A pregnancy results when a male sperm unites with a female egg in the Fallopian tube, with the fertilised egg implanting in the lining of the uterus. Infertility occurs when this process breaks down at any stage. There are many causes of infertility, but by far the most common are deficient sperm production, problems of tubal transport of either sperm or fertilised egg, and defects in ovulation (egg production). At present it is possible to find the reason for infertility in only 90% of infertile couples.

Discovering the cause requires a detailed history and physical examination by a doctor and then a series of tests. Usually the only test for the male is to produce a specimen of semen for analysis – the 'sperm count'. This analysis determines whether the semen volume and the number, movement and shape of the sperm are normal. Tests for the female include temperature charts and blood and urine tests to assess whether ovulation is occurring, a dye x-ray (hysterosalpingogram) and laparoscopy (a telescope passed into the abdomen) to assess patency of the Fallopian tubes and cervical mucus tests.

Treatment is more successful for women than men. If an abnormality in ovulation is causing infertility then drugs to stimulate egg production are often successful. Tubal problems may occasionally be improved by surgery but otherwise one of two techniques is usually used: either in-vitro fertilisation and embryo transfer (IVF and ET) which involves fertilising the egg in a laboratory and replacing the embryo into the uterus or gamete intrafallopian transfer (GIFT) mixing sperm and egg in the laboratory and replacing the mixture into the Fallopian tube. If sperm transport is the problem then high intrauterine insemination (IUI) which involves placing sperm into the upper uterus at the time of ovulation may be successful. Treatment for the male is much less successful and in this situation many doctors would recommend artificial insemination using donor sperm (AID), although intracyloplasmic sperm injection (ICSI), whereby sperm are injected directly into the egg, has improved fertilisation rates more recently.

The Bible has much to say on the issue of infertility. Firstly in the Old Testament children are seen as a gift of God and a blessing (Genesis 1:28, 9:7), often as a blessing of obedience (Deut 7:12-14, 28:11; Psalm 113:9; 127:3-5; 128:2-4). On the other hand 'barrenness' or infertility is seen as a curse and a cause of great pain and suffering. (Deut 28:18).

This must be balanced by the blessing of God's grace to childless couples. As the Psalmist says 'He settles the barren woman in her home as a happy mother of children' (Psalm 113:9). The Bible gives many accounts of childless couples where God's grace intervened (often in response to prayer) and children eventually came after a time of agonised waiting. Often these

children were particularly strategic in God's plan – the pregnancies of Rachel (Gen 30:2), Rebekah (Gen 25:21), Sarai (Gen 16:1,2,5), Hannah (1 Sam 1), Elizabeth (Luke 1:7), Manoah's wife (Judges 13:2,3) and, of course, Mary (Matt 1:18) are obvious examples.

There are two mistakes Christians make in applying these Scriptures. One is to assume that all infertility is the result of sin that the couple have committed and the other is to assume that it never is. While it is true that some infertility does result directly from personal sin (e.g. tubal disease often is the result of sexually transmitted infection which may occur when people break God's law of one man, one woman for life) it is not true that this is always so. Infertility does not imply that the couple affected are any worse sinners than those who are not (Luke 13:1-5). The spiritual cause of much infertility is a mystery. God has His reasons which reason cannot know and it is dangerous for us to speculate in these circumstances. We should rather rest content knowing that 'in all things God works for the good of those who love Him' (Rom 8:28). Sometimes Christian couples may even choose not to have children for

the purpose of devoting themselves more unreservedly to God's service (Luke 23:29).

For Christian couples who are infertile the decision whether or not to seek medical help must be made. The importance of prayer first and foremost cannot be overstated. However, if medical help is sought (and God can often work through doctors in this way) the most important question is whether the end justifies the means. Childlessness can be very distressing for the couple involved, but this does not mean that a child is to be sought at any price.

There are several problems for Christians in the whole area of infertility treatments. Firstly, sperm for a sperm count is produced by masturbation. Is this morally permissible in the right context? Is using donor sperm or a donor egg a violation of the marriage bond and therefore adultery?

Many in-vitro fertilisation programmes involve such techniques as freezing of embryos, experimentation on embryos, discarding of embryos surplus to requirement or routine amniocentesis and possible abortion. For this reason many Christians who take the view that life begins at fertilisation would feel

that IVF is only permissible in limited circumstances (i.e. when all embryos produced are re-implanted at the time most likely to ensure survival). This is, of course, not a problem with GIFT. Also the investigation and treatment of infertility is very expensive and for some types of infertility, has a very low success rate. Is it then morally justified?

For those couples who are unable to conceive, even with medical help, or who find that they have moral reservations about the techniques involved, adoption remains the best option. There is a good biblical basis for this as God's way of providing, both for the desire of an infertile couple for a child and for the need of a parentless child for a home. Adoption is, after all, what God does for us when we become Christians (Rom 8:14,15,23; 9:4; Gal 4:27) and we are enjoined to love in the same way that Christ has loved us (John 13:34,35), and to care for orphans (James 1:27). It is ironical that the number of children available for adoption is falling, largely as a result of abortion and increased government support for unmarried mothers, at a time when the demand is increasing.

© *Christian Medical Fellowship (CMF)*

The death of natural procreation

A brief survey of reproduction technologies which threaten natural procreation

A. *Three Generations of IVF*

In some ways Louise Brown represents something of a technological museum piece. She was simply the first successful experiment in a series of 103 attempts to create a baby in a petri dish and then transfer him or her to the mother's womb.

By 1992 when Chloe O'Brien was born the technology had moved on. Chloe's mother and father were both carriers of a single copy of a defective gene for cystic fibrosis. Both parents knew that one child in four conceived by them would be affected

By Peter Garrett, MA, Research & Education Director for LIFE

by cystic fibrosis – with all that would mean in lung infections, tissue damage, infertility problems and a reduced life-span. They also knew that two in every four of the children would be carriers of the defective gene, just as they themselves were. Only one in four of their naturally conceived children would carry two good copies of the gene and be at risk neither of having the condition nor of passing it on to their own children.

Mr and Mrs O'Brien were put in touch with Professor Robert Winston at the Hammersmith Hospital in London. He was involved in a new technique known as pre-implantation diagnosis (P.I.D.) and was using genetic tests to de-select all those test-tube babies who didn't make the grade. By employing this form of laboratory eugenics, Robert Winston ensured that those affected by the condition cystic fibrosis were de-selected, along with those which would have been carriers of the single copy of the defective gene. Ironically those children with genotypes (genetic constitutions) similar to those of the parents didn't qualify for

29

the right to spend nine months in their own mother's womb.

Throughout the 1990s the death rate for embryos produced in this country has been around 97%. As we expand the range of genetic tests, and as we incorporate the information derived from the multi-billion dollar Human Genome Project, the death rate will rise inexorably towards 100%. In other words, it will become almost impossible for a test-tube baby to pass the genetic tests and qualify for the right to develop in his/her own mother's womb. This is the future of IVF.

B. Surrogacy

Surrogacy will become more common in the 21st century as it links up with other new reproductive technologies such as cloning. Surrogacy will continue to produce a flood of horrifying stories of neglect and abandonment, as well as occasionally generating situations in which the parties to the surrogacy agreement end up fighting over whether the baby should live or die. Three case studies clearly illustrate such outcomes.

One woman from Texas by the name of Denise responded to an advert for surrogate mothers placed in a supermarket tabloid magazine. It seemed like the perfect solution to her debt problems. Unfortunately, Denise's heart condition was not discovered by her doctor until she was six months pregnant. In spite of pleading with a cardiologist to find the cause of her rapid heart-beat and breathlessness, her calls for help didn't result in a proper investigation. She was unable to find the $250 she needed to buy the heart monitor which her doctor advised her to wear, and the baby broker offered no help at all. In the eighth month of the pregnancy, just twenty-five days from the baby's due date, she was found dead in bed with her unborn son nestled inside her womb. The bodies of mother and baby were sent to Denise's mother who buried them on her farm. Denise's mother never heard from the brokers or the contracting couple (taken from *Living Laboratories* by Robyn Rowland).

In another high-profile repro-tech case from California, Jaycee Buzzanca, was declared motherless and fatherless after a judge analysed the technological novelties in her conception and gestation. Donor sperm and donor eggs had been used to create Jaycee in the laboratory. She was then transferred to the womb of a surrogate mother. During the pregnancy the commissioning couple, who had paid the equivalent of £6,250 for Jaycee, separated. The commissioning 'father' successfully avoided paying maintenance by arguing that Jaycee was not his in any legal sense. In ruling in favour of Mr Buzzanca the judge also observed that Mrs Buzzanca was not legally Jaycee's mother either.

Surrogacy will become more common in the 21st century as it links up with other new reproductive technologies such as cloning

---

This case strongly resembles that of 10-year-old Stephanie Bloor, who was conceived by anonymous insemination. In 1995, she was financially disowned by the man she called Daddy, who, following a divorce from Stephanies's mother, refused to pay child support because he wasn't her father. Prior to the divorce Stephanie's real origins had been kept from her.

Stephanie and Jaycee are the real victims in all this, as the runaway repro-tech industry creates endless new variations upon the common theme that adults quarrel and 'their' children suffer.

Sometimes disagreements between the commissioning couple and the surrogate mother come to focus upon whether the baby should live or die. In one famous case the surrogate mother went for a pre-natal scan and was told that the baby was affected by Down's Syndrome. When she communicated this news to the commissioning couple they told her to have an abortion. When the surrogate mother objected by saying that she was against abortion, the couple told her that she would not be having her abortion, but rather that she would be having an abortion for them – in effect an abortion by proxy. Eventually the surrogate mother agreed to their request. To this day she believes that she had their abortion and not hers. Such cases have a devastating psychological impact on the surrogate mother, and they confirm that modern repro-tech commercialises motherhood, commodifies babies and denatures humanity.

C. Spermatogonia transplantation

Another threat to natural procreation is that posed by spermatogonia transplantation. This technique was originally developed for race horses and is intended to enable prize stallions such as, for example, Red

Rum (3-time winner of the Grand National) to sire or father larger numbers of foals without having to travel to stud farms all over the country. The idea is to remove some of the tissue from the testes of the stallion donors and then transplant it into spaces created in the testes of other stallions. In one version of the treatment just part of the recipient's spermatogonia tissue is destroyed using a laser before the new material from the donor is implanted. This particular procedure results in hybrid sperm populations in which some are genetically derived from the donor and others are genetically derived from the recipient's own cells. To ensure that all offspring are genetically related to the donor it is necessary to use the laser to burn out all the spermatogonia tissue in the recipients' testes. When the two scientists who developed this technique applied for a patent in 1992 they concluded their applications by looking forward to the human applications of this technology.

With spermatogonia transplantation the invasion of the relationship between husband and wife is different from that envisaged in artificial insemination by donor (AID). In fact, some commentators have argued that spermatogonia transplantation is preferable, because at least the husband (recipient) is involved in the conception of the child, even if the child conceived is not genetically related to him.

In the hands of a dictator this technology could be employed with sinister effect. What if it became compulsory for all men to submit to this treatment? What if the dictator's spermatogonia tissue was proliferated in a laboratory and then implanted into the testes of all adult males? Such a scenario may not be that far-fetched, as we've already witnessed clinic directors at sperm banks and test-tube baby centres using their own sperm instead of that provided by husbands and donors. These people are simply driven by the Darwinian idea that biological success is the ability to produce offspring in large numbers.

D. Egg-fusion
Scientists in America working with the egg cells of mice have found a way to solve one aspect of what is known as the imprinting problem. In the past scientists have been unable to fertilise an egg because the genes derived from these 'identical' sources have refused to 'communicate' with each other. Clearly, something in the genetic chemistry of the cell nuclei tells the genes if they derive from a male or a female parent.

The idea of sex without babies (contraception) soon leads on to babies without sex (IVF). Why should we now be surprised that babies without parents – human clones – are about to be born?

Now, scientists have found a way to switch off these genetic blocking devices, and have persuaded the egg nuclei to fuse and form an embryo. It is estimated that this technique will take two years to transfer from mice to people. When this technology transfer is accomplished it will allow lesbian mothers to have children which are equally related to each of them. This option may prove more attractive than the cloning option because the 'parenthood' is not asymmetric as it would be in the case of cloning. One thing is certain, the redundancy of the male is assured.

E. Male pregnancy
Men need not despair because, just as technology is providing ways for women to have children without men, so technology is suggesting ways in which men may themselves become mothers.

In a recent article about 'male motherhood', Lord Winston argued: 'Male pregnancy would certainly be possible and would be the same as when a woman has an ectopic pregnancy – outside the uterus – although to sustain it, you'd have to give the man lots of female hormones' (*The Sunday Times*, 21.2.99). In fact, in Australia at least five male homosexual couples have already applied for this so-called 'treatment'. The applicants have always been rejected, usually on safety grounds. In the early 1990s it was thought that such male pregnancies might kill up to 50% of the 'father-mothers'. Lord Winston seems confident that close medical supervision could reduce the fatality statistics to acceptable levels.

Dr Simon Fishel, director of the Centre For Assisted Reproduction in Nottingham, agrees. He has said, 'There is no reason why a man could not carry a child. The placenta provides the necessary hormonal conditions, so it doesn't have to be inside a woman.'

Conclusion
The bringing into being of men and women has remained unchanged since time immemorial. Two became one flesh. Then, out of their union, as gifts ever new, their sons and daughters were created. In our own time we have learned to separate the union in sexual intimacy from the conception of children. The idea of sex without babies (contraception) soon leads on to babies without sex (IVF). Why should we now be surprised that babies without parents – human clones – are about to be born? The arena of natural procreation has been flooded by a continuous stream of technological innovation. IVF, surrogacy, and artificial insemination have now been joined by sperma-togonial transplants, egg-fusion (fatherless babies), male pregnancies and at the apex of the post-pro-creative technologies – human cloning itself.

There is a relentless drive towards quality control and total product management, as the language of the production line has invaded the realm of human procreation. In the near future it may come to be considered irresponsible to resort to natural procreation without a battery of pre-natal tests being employed. The modern citizen of the near future may learn to be angry when confronted with the spectacle of a less than perfect baby. 'Didn't you know you could have had that thing tested for abnormality?' Could this be the gentle rebuke of a concerned citizen in the face of a mother whose child is affected by Downs Syndrome? Is it really possible to maintain the current schizophrenia, which offers extra help and support to those already born with special needs, while seeking out and destroying those, with the same special needs, who have yet to be born? New forms of discrimination will emerge and children will learn to distinguish one another not according to age or skin colour, but according to the manner in which they came into the world. Might not those produced by IVF (with genetic testing) come to be viewed as a class apart? Will not those produced by way of cloning become the victims of discrimination? The echo of the alphas and deltas in Aldous Huxley's *Brave New World* is all too clear.

All of this lies shrouded in the mists of the 21st century. All of it will shape what we become. But whatever the future, the coming to be of men and women will never be the same again. The idea of accepting a child unconditionally, regardless of perfection or imperfection, is gone for ever. Gone too is the contingency and uncertainty of human procreation which traditionally underpinned the 'radical equality' of children and their parents; because that which is planned and ordered into being cannot be equal to that which does the planning and ordering.

We must conclude by viewing ourselves from afar. From such a vantage point we find ourselves rushing towards a technological embrace, and we come to understand the truth of the quotation: love of the future begins where other loves end. We will become faster, richer, smarter, but at the price of being less than we were, less alive, less truly human. We are in fact witnessing nothing less than the animalisation of mankind. The reproductive technologies of the farmyard are threatening to eclipse natural procreation and to obliterate a central component of human personhood. Only a renewed effort to explore the significance of the human body and of human procreative sexuality will provide adequate protection against this accelerating dehumanisation.

© *LIFE*

A dangerous path

We are the first society in history to sever the connection between sex and procreation. It is a dangerous path indeed down which we now tread . . .

Here is a story of our time. A rich Italian businessman and his Portuguese wife wanted a third child. They already had two, produced by surrogacy, and they wanted to repeat the process.

So they went to an agency in Denmark which found them the type of donor they wanted (tall, athletic, blond, but Latin-looking).

The sperm donor came from the US. The egg donor lives in Britain, as does the surrogate mother. She is a working-class woman from the West Midlands, and had already acted as a surrogate three times before. One of the earlier surrogate babies had been aborted because of various abnormalities. She also had two children of her own, by two different men.

This new surrogacy operation was performed in Athens. After more than 21 weeks of pregnancy it emerged that, instead of the boy the prospective parents had really wanted, the surrogate mother was carrying twin girls. The would-be parents demanded an abortion, but she refused. Nor did she want the babies to go into care.

By Anthony O'Hear

So she looked for a couple to adopt the twins. After many difficulties, one was found: a lesbian couple living in Hollywood. Julia Salazar and Tracey Stern. The twins, Emma and Danielle, are now in Hollywood and are being looked after by a nanny from Puerto Rico.

Astonishing

The birth mother is deeply unhappy because there is no real contact between her and the twins who occupied her womb before they were born.

Truly a story of our time – a story of astonishing medical procedures, which could not have been performed at any other time. But a story, also, of astonishing human selfishness, muddle and unhappiness. And a story whose complexities are really only just beginning.

A story in which, almost certainly, yet more tragedy and heartache will compound that which has already occurred.

A story in which children are treated as if they were commodities or a sort of fashion statement. A story in which children are produced to satisfy adult vanity and desire. A story in which they are got rid of if they do not come up to scratch.

A story in which natural affections of birth mothers and of children are treated as of no consequence. And all this is before Danielle and Emma have been on Earth for a year.

But just who are Danielle and Emma? Whose children are they? What is their nationality? Who are their parents? Do they have any grandparents?

We could spend months discussing all these questions, so vital to our identity and happiness, without ever coming up with a decisive answer.

And who, at the end of the day, will look after them? Who is, ultimately, responsible for them? Who will really care for them? What sort of a life will they have?

In the normal state of affairs there are simple answers to all these questions. Children are the children of their biological parents: that is, those who have conceived them in a normal sexual relationship, which is normally sanctified and legally recognised by marriage.

The biological parents will bring up the children, love them and care for them, probably with love and help from grandparents. And the children will have a life their parents understand and prepare them for.

As it is fashionable now to scoff at this very normal scenario, let us consider its singular advantage. In it, in the most beautiful way possible, social arrangements follow and enhance nature.

In the traditional family, the biological bonds and natural affections between parents and offspring are cemented in the social bonds which tie the family together and support it in times of trouble. And the family itself reflects the needs of all the parties. It reflects the needs of the child, who requires many years of care and attention.

It reflects the needs of the mother, who requires the support of the father. And it reflects the needs of the father, giving him the social role and standing which follow from his parental responsibilities.

Of course, children can be brought up successfully outside a normal marriage, and not all normal marriages are successful. But that does not imply we should deliberately engineer situations in which the tried and tested norm is flouted.

Selfish

But that is just what we are doing today, with the consequences we see in the case of Danielle and Emma. And, unless we call a halt very soon, things are going to get more complicated, with yet more tragedy and uncertainty.

We are told that, within the next 20 or 30 years, it will be commonplace for women to store their eggs before the age of 30, for them to choose sperm from donors who fit their ideal specifications, for them actually to produce their children – or have them produced by someone else – when they are in their 60s, or later.

There will be clones and vats full of eggs and embryos, waiting on the convenience of selfish adults, to be used or thrown away at will.

Danielle and Emma are simply precursors of this brave new world. We are the first society to attempt to sever the connection between sex and procreation. And we are doing it in both directions, so to speak.

It is exactly 40 years since the contraceptive pill was introduced. In the US it has been used by 80 per cent of the women born since 1946. We can all now freely engage in sexual activity in the reasonable certainty that there will be no children.

We are clearly moving to a situation in which children are created to some ideal specification and only loosely connected to those from whom they receive their genes

---

Sex itself is sold as pure recreation, with women as 'laddish' as men. No doubt, psychologically and emotionally this is damaging, for deep down in our nature the link between sexual desire and the desire for children remains strong.

LOOK - YOU'VE GOT THE BEST GENES MONEY COULD BUY!!

...WOULD'VE BEEN HAPPY WITH THE ONES THAT CAME FOR FREE...

Importance

But arguably even more damaging is production of children outside a sexual relationship, as we see in the case of Emma and Danielle. For that strikes at the roots of the most fundamental social bond, that between biological parents and the children of their love.

In this bond, the children then become the recipients not just of the love of their parents, but also of a secure identity, linked to the wider family of grandparents and earlier generations.

All this, whose importance can hardly be overestimated, is simply being thrown away by the new reproductive technologies and the morality which seems to accompany them.

If nothing else, the story of Danielle and Emma has the merit of illustrating the world we are preparing for ourselves and our children.

We are clearly moving to a situation in which children are created to some ideal specification and only loosely connected to those from whom they receive their genes. That is, if the genes are not themselves produced in the laboratory.

The next move will doubtless be not just artificial conception and fertilisation, but the whole of gestation in some clinically-controlled situation.

Will the children thus produced belong to anyone? Or will the state, or some private agency, regulate their creation and upbringing? Will there be baby farms where designer parents can select their ready-made designer babies?

All this may seem fantastic now, but 20 years ago could anyone have imagined the story of Danielle and Emma?

Before we proceed further into the world in which Danielle and Emma themselves will grow up, shouldn't we now stop the developments which allowed them to be born?

• Anthony O'Hear is Professor of Philosophy at Bradford University. This article first appeared in *The Daily Mail*, May 2000.

© Professor Anthony O'Hear

'Faceless fathers' may be identified

By Cherry Norton,
Social Affairs Editor

Ministers are to consider creating a separate birth register for children conceived by anonymous sperm donation, allowing details of their true origins to become officially available for the first time.

The plan would force thousands of parents to tell their children about their genetic heritage, as it would be written on their birth certificates and would remove the secrecy that surrounds conception through assisted reproduction. The proposal is one of five options drawn up by the Department of Health to deal with the issue of donor insemination, which will be presented to ministers in the next two weeks. A public consultation document will be produced shortly. In Britain, more than 10,000 children have been born using donor insemination (DI) since 1991. Last year 1,349 babies were born using the technique.

Nearly all of these children have no idea of their origins, because more than 90 per cent of parents who conceive a child using sperm from an unknown male donor do not tell them that their 'social father' is not the genetic father.

Research has shown that most parents are worried that telling the truth will undermine the child's relationship with the social father. But many psychologists believe the damage caused by family secrets can be far more devastating.

Children conceived by donor sperm have a birth certificate that identifies their social father but does not give any indication of the intervention of medical technology or any clues as to their real origins.

Giving children the right to trace their genetic fathers, in a similar way that adopted children were given the right to find their biological parents in the 1970s, is the most controversial option under consideration.

Changes in the law could also mean that men would only be able to give sperm if they were willing to be identified to any future children.

Health experts have criticised any removal of the anonymity of sperm donors, saying that it will destroy the fertility industry and lead to an acute shortage of sperm for infertile couples.

> ## Changes in the law could also mean that men would only be able to give sperm if they were willing to be identified to any future children

A spokesman for the Department of Health confirmed: 'The options being considered range from the status quo to complete disclosure of all information.'

Since 1991, all clinics doing fertility work must be registered with the Human Fertilisation and Embryology Authority, and all sperm donors give basic information – name, national insurance number, known medical history and hobbies and interests.

The DI offspring have no right to access this information, although they are told, if they are intending to marry, whether or not their future spouse is a half brother or sister.

Supporters of a separate register for donor insemination children say that this lack of honesty about someone's origins leads to long-term social and emotional problems. Those who are never told often suffer from identity crises. Those who are told may feel frustrated, because they are blocked from finding out further information about their genetic roots.

Six DI adults have spoken to The Independent. They said depriving them of the right to know was an abuse of human rights. Many were not told until adulthood. A spokesman for the Donor Conception network, which encourages parents to tell their children about their origins, said that a separate register for DI children was the 'right moral stance'.

But Tim Hegley, a spokesman for Issue, a charity that supports infertile couples, asked: 'Why should infertile couples be forced to reveal things that fertile couples are not?'

© The Independent
April, 2000

Should sperm donors be traceable?

Yes: Elizabeth Wincott, Program Group on Assisted Reproduction
No: Tim Hedgley, Issue, National Fertility Association

Dear Tim,

With a government consultation paper due within weeks on parental anonymity, the starting point has to be this: more than 6,000 people are born each year as a result of a growing range of reproductive techniques. They are currently the only group in this country who don't have the right in law to trace their genetic parents – a fundamental violation of their human rights.

Although adoption isn't entirely analogous, it was recognised some years ago that adoptive children need to have the right to trace their natural parents. Why should they be denied?

This denial creates a climate where secrecy about origins can flourish, which can be very damaging, since information often emerges in an unplanned way that can cause huge emotional distress.

Legislating for the right to trace parents doesn't necessarily mean people will take up the option. But we must allow for the possibility. The law should be changed – prospectively – as soon as possible.

Yours sincerely,
Elizabeth Wincott, Program Group on Assisted Reproduction

Dear Elizabeth,

We need to appreciate the scale of this. In 1996/97 there were 6,978 people born as a result of licensed reproductive techniques. That means 6,978 people who had successful treatment. Many of them will have partners and families who also feel the joy of conceiving after a long, distressing and painful period of trying for a baby. It is our view that the child, the recipient and the donor deserve equal care under the law.

We believe the donor and recipient also have rights – rights to privacy that would have to be set aside if the current proposal to remove donor anonymity were to become law.

First, it is necessary to remove the need for secrecy that surrounds infertility. One in seven couples in this country have difficulty in conceiving, but are still sufficiently stigmatised by this medical condition to want to keep it secret. Removing the social, cultural and religious grounds for that secrecy would be a good first step. Then there could be openness – provided all parties agreed.

I donated sperm to assist another couple become parents of 'their child'. I did not donate sperm to become a father again. I have two children; I do not want any more. Even though the law as proposed would not be retrospective, I know that if I had been faced with the same situation today, knowing that my details would be made available to the child and the recipient, I would not have gone ahead.

Who knows how many couples suffering the distress of infertility would not now be experiencing the joy of raising children as a result?

Yours, Tim Hedgley,
Chair, Issue, the National Fertility Association

Dear Tim,

I fully agree with you that the need for secrecy that surrounds infertility needs to be lifted. One way of doing

> **Legislating for the right to trace parents doesn't necessarily mean people will take up the option. But we must allow for the possibility**

this is by the debate we and others are having in public – but this needs to be developed more widely. I in no way want to suggest that recipients' and donors' rights should be set aside. They, and people born as a result of donation, have rights that should be carefully considered and preserved.

But donors and recipients are adults, who have choices. They may, after advice and counselling, decide to pursue assistance with conception – or they may choose to adopt or foster. Some choose to have no children at all.

People donate sperm or eggs for a variety of reasons. There is evidence to suggest that, in countries where anonymity has been lifted, donors still come forward. I'm not suggesting that donors should ever have financial responsibilities as parents. But they should understand that at some point in the future a young person born as a result of their donation may wish to seek contact with them.

It's important that this process is thought through carefully at the time of donation, with the assistance of a trained counsellor. A possible meeting may seem remote at the time of donation – but it's important for donors to prepare themselves in advance. So long as the terms under which a donor donates and a recipient receives are made clear, there is, I believe, no violation of their rights.

With good wishes,
Elizabeth

Dear Elizabeth,

Recipients may have the choices you mention – but at present too many still can't make the best one: to have their own child with their own egg and their partner's sperm.

This outcome is becoming increasingly possible through IVF

and intracytoplasmic sperm injection (ICSI), where a single sperm is injected directly into the egg. In the future, the principal groups of people who would still need donor insemination would be those wishing to avoid passing on an inherited disease, or those whose sperm have been irreparably damaged. But if funding for ICSI or IVF is not available, donor insemination becomes the only alternative within the financial reach of many couples. It is not unusual for patients to need three or four cycles of IVF treatment before conceiving – and at £1,500 to £2,000 a cycle, that's not an easy choice.

As the law stands, donors have no responsibilities for children born as a result of their donation – but they have no rights to them either. We believe that the balance between rights and responsibilities underpins the progress of civilisation. Surely changing the law would give children rights where they could not have balancing responsibilities? The natural corollary to that must be that the genetic father could in turn demand access and other rights to his child. Or do such rights only work one way?

In countries where anonymity has been removed, the age of the donors has substantially increased, leading to problems with the quality of the sperm. If a donor wishes to make it clear that he gives on condition that he remain anonymous, shouldn't his right be protected?

Best wishes, Tim

Dear Tim,
I agree there should be a balance between rights and responsibilities, but the issue of choice comes in again here. Adults, whether infertile couples or potential donors, have choices. With support and counselling they can work through the implications of the choices they make.

But people born through assisted conception have no choice. They do not ask to be born. As responsible adults, we have to ensure a balance between fairness for such people and the wishes of members of the medical profession, infertile couples and

donors. It's significant that a growing number of individuals born using IVF are articulating their concern for those yet to be born, knowing that they themselves may never have that option: records associated with their biological parentage no longer exist in many cases.

If the law is changed, positive publicity is likely to result in different kinds of donors – but careful screening can ensure the quality of the sperm. A donor who wished to remain anonymous after the law was changed would clearly be precluded from donating. But that's surely a small price to pay compared to the distress experienced by some donor offspring.

Anonymity needs to be lifted prospectively as soon as possible.

Yours, Elizabeth

Dear Elizabeth,
People born without assisted conception don't ask to be born either. They have no choice as to their biological parents, and their parents have had no counselling over their choice to have a child. It seems unreasonable to erect unnecessary barriers for those

---

We believe the donor and recipient also have rights – rights to privacy

---

going through the trauma of assisted conception when such barriers don't exist for those who don't need treatment.

I suggest we learn from recent changes to the law regarding adoption. There, where the child has supposedly been put at the centre, there are stories of families being torn apart when an adopted child seeks out its biological parents. These attempts to do good have led to untold misery.

With the children of assisted conception, there has been no rejection, only a medical condition that did not respond to treatment.

I hope that my sperm donation has helped to give several couples the joy of a child. I know those parents will raise that child as their own. I believe the security that child will feel as a consequence of being born into a safe environment may not overcome their curiosity, but there will not be the same need to know who I am as there would be if I were an absent father.

Let's lay the foundations for every child to be a wanted child; every child to be given the respect and dignity of a caring home; and for every couple that wants a child to have equal access to the treatment that will make that possible. Now there's a law worth making!

Regards, Tim

This foolish threat to the gift of life

By Lord Robert Winston

The Government is reported to be considering whether to give many thousands of so-called 'test-tube' children the right to trace their biological parents.

Quite right, too, you may think. There is nothing shameful about being a donor or the child of a donor. Indeed, the act of giving sperm or eggs ought to be seen as noble and selfless, and the fact that the legal parents went through such effort to have a child is a strong signal that the child was desperately wanted and is deeply loved.

You do not have IVF children by accident. So why the cloak of secrecy? What is there to hide?

The legal reformers also point out that ours is an age of openness, and that children who have been adopted were given the right to trace their biological parents many years ago.

Most of us think this was a wise and humane decision. So why not extend it to IVF children?

But, as someone who has worked in the field of infertility, using donated sperm or eggs for many years, the prospect of a further change in the law fills me with concern. Without the most careful assessment first, a change in the law could damage the chances of many people to have a family, and cause more distress than it would cure.

Many donors give their sperm or eggs only on the strict understanding that their generous act will remain anonymous – a guarantee which we can give them today in good faith – though, since 1991, clinics have been forced by the Government to keep records on donors.

For understandable reasons, few donors relish the prospect of a young stranger accosting them years later and possibly demanding an explanation, or even a relationship with them. Some may fear that the Child Support Agency might start chasing them for money.

If we cannot guarantee potential donors that cloak of anonymity, then undoubtedly these donors would be harder to find. And if the right to trace biological parents were to be made retrospective it would be an utterly deplorable breach of confidence.

These are not hypothetical worries. When similar legislation was passed in Sweden in 1984 the number of donors – sperm donors, in particular – dropped sharply, though I accept that figures eventually began to pick up again.

> ## Few donors relish the prospect of a young stranger accosting them years later and possibly demanding an explanation, or even a relationship with them

Anything which scares off donors without very good reason is surely to be deplored at a time when demand for fertility treatment is growing.

Every day hospitals, including my own, have to turn away serious and responsible would-be parents because the necessary sperm or eggs are not available. We should not make this sorry situation worse unless we can clearly show that children born from these relationships are emotionally damaged by not knowing their donor parents.

Why should society impose further and unnecessary delays on couples desperate for children?

The answer we are given is that many children born as a result of sperm or egg donation are growing up desperately anxious to know who their biological father or mother was. If this could be proved it would be a powerful argument.

I know that, for me – as a practitioner – the feelings of the child are overwhelmingly important. I do not want to bring a generation of unhappy, damaged and disturbed children into the world.

That is not part of my job description. It was not why I chose to specialise in the treatment of infertility. If solid evidence were ever produced which persuaded me that this was what I was doing, I would stop.

But the truth of the matter is that those who want to change the law have virtually no academic evidence to support their emotional or ideological case for openness. The research simply has not been carried out.

Of course, the reformers can tell of the odd case of a child who is unhappy about not being able to trace the sperm or egg donor who made his or her birth possible.

It goes without saying that any such case distresses me deeply. But I can match them ten to one with stories of happy families and contented youngsters who feel no sense of loss or deprivation.

As long as the legal parents explain gradually and positively the circumstances of a child's birth, from an early age, there seems very little evidence that there should be a problem.

This is the point at which those who favour a change in the law fall back on an attempt to make comparisons with adopted children, some of whom undoubtedly want to find their biological parents.

Indeed, it was largely because of the driving determination of Phillip Whitehead (then an MP, now an MEP) to trace his biological parents, that the law was changed in 1975.

We all remember the delight of both Clare Short and the son she gave up for adoption when they were reunited last year.

So perhaps blood (or genetic material) really is thicker than water. Perhaps donor-insemination children feel as disturbed as some adopted children apparently do by not knowing their biological parents.

But there is no real parallel between adoption and sperm or egg donation. Indeed, there is a vital difference. Adoption can often involve deep psychological feelings of guilt and rejection. The mother who gives up her child after much agonising, in the strong and correct belief that she is doing the right thing for her baby, may still feel guilt and a sense of loss.

The child who is happily adopted into a family he or she loves and trusts, may still feel distress about being 'rejected' by his biological mother.

Those feelings may only be assuaged by a meeting between biological parent and child. I do not find it easy to accept that IVF treatment carries the same psychological baggage.

So I say to the Government: there is no need for rushed legislation which will undoubtedly make it more difficult for childless couples to have donor treatment.

Instead, it is time for some serious research into whether 'test-tube' children face special problems. Then, and only then, should we consider changing the law.

● Lord Robert Winston, was talking to John Torode. This article first appeared in *The Daily Mail*, July 1999.

© Lord Robert Winston

The battle to join the test-tube baby boom

Homosexual couples may win the right to demand test-tube babies under the new human rights law, the head of the Government's fertility watchdog said yesterday.

Gays, lesbians, single women and those over 60 are likely to try to use the Human Rights Act to overturn rules which effectively bar anyone but heterosexual couples under the age of 40 from receiving in-vitro fertilisation treatment through the NHS.

Ruth Deech, chairman of the Human Fertilisation and Embryology Authority, said that couples might also use the new law to insist on a right to choose the sex of a baby.

Her prediction comes amid growing fears over the impact of the act, which incorporates the European Convention on Human Rights into English law from October and gives judges the power to decide whether English legislation meets the requirements of the Euro-charter.

Critics say it will allow them huge scope to overrule Parliament and make their own law.

In Scotland, where the new human rights regime has already gone into operation, judges have already sprung a series of surprises on Ministers. One ruling has declared the use of cameras to catch speeding drivers illegal and threatens to

By Steve Doughty, Social Affairs Correspondent

undermine the policing of speed limits by cameras unworkable throughout Britain.

Mrs Deech said fertility law governing test-tube pregnancies is likely to be one of the first battle grounds. 'I suspect that from October we're going to have a lot of interesting questions being raised about whether treatment can be refused to single women, to women of 60, to lesbian and gay couples, to widows, and whether sex selection for social reasons can be denied,' she said.

'I think people will come forward and say, "I want this; I have a right to private and family life, I have a right to marry and found a family". The courts may reject the more far-fetched claims, but they may have to consider them.'

In an interview with The *Guardian*, she added: 'If a single

'I think people will come forward and say, "I want this; I have a right to private and family life

woman were rejected for treatment by a clinic, she might say, "I demand my human rights".

'If a lesbian couple, perhaps, had a baby abroad or were rejected by a clinic here, they would challenge any refusal to treat them like a heterosexual couple, because there is a clause which says the rights and liberties in this act must be extended to people without discrimination as to status.

'I am not saying all the careful protection we have will crumble but it seems to be likely that some very deep questions will be posed to the courts.'

Current legislation says no woman should have test-tube treatment 'unless account has been taken of the welfare of any child who may be born as a result (including the need of that child for a father) and of any other child who may be affected by the birth'.

It also says a doctor must consider the ability of prospective parents 'to provide a stable and supportive environment for any child', together with their ages and their long-term ability to meet a child's needs.

Single women, gays, lesbians and older women have received IVF from private clinics but NHS clinics almost invariably give treatment only to stable heterosexual couples under 40.

© The Daily Mail February, 2000

Human rights test for fertility rules

By Sarah Boseley, Lucy Ward and Julia Hartley Brewer

Human rights legislation which comes into force this autumn will lead to a spate of legal challenges by single women, older women, gay men and others who believe existing fertility rules have denied them the right to have a family, the chair of the Human Fertilisation and Embryology Authority has predicted.

Home office sources last night acknowledged that the new human rights act could lead to a string of test cases over fertility issues, as individuals opt to challenge the current rules in the courts.

In an interview with the *Guardian*, Ruth Deech, who has worked as an international lawyer, said: 'I suspect that from October we're going to have a lot of interesting questions being raised about whether treatment can be refused to single women, to women of 60, to lesbian and gay couples, to widows, and whether sex selection for social reasons can be denied.'

The human rights legislation which is being introduced from Europe was originally a response to the atrocities committed in Nazi Germany. 'To make sure there was never again the forced sterilisation of men and women, it has got provisions like the right to private and family life; the right to marry and found a family. Those two rights are rooted in the horrors of the second world war – the prohibition of sexual relations between people of different races,' Ms Deech said.

In modern Britain, however, those phrases are open to another interpretation – that no one who wants a child should be denied the chance to have one, regardless of sexual orientation, age or anything else.

'I think people will come forward and say, "I want this; I have a right to private and family life, I have a right to marry and found a family." The courts may reject the more far-fetched claims, but they may have to consider them,' Ms Deech said.

'If a single woman were rejected for treatment by a clinic, she might say, "I demand my human rights". If a lesbian couple, perhaps, had a baby abroad or were rejected by a clinic here, they would challenge any refusal to treat them like a heterosexual couple, because there is a clause which says the rights and liberties in this act must be extended to people without discrimination as to status. I'm not saying that all the careful protection we have will crumble, but it seems to be likely that some very deep questions will be posed to the courts.'

> *. . . no one who wants a child should be denied the chance to have one, regardless of sexual orientation, age or anything else*

The human rights legislation is not supposed to override British statute but it will be for the courts to try to strike a balance. One of the conditions of a licence granted by the HFEA to a clinic to practise in-vitro fertilisation is that 'a woman shall not be provided with treatment unless account has been taken of the welfare of any child who may be born as a result (including the need of that child for a father), and of any other child who may be affected by the birth'. But the meaning of that phrase is 'terribly unclear', said Ms Deech

No category of woman is specifically excluded from treatment by the regulations, so in principle a single woman, older woman or lesbian couple can be treated. But the HFEA lays down specific factors to be considered by the doctor, including 'their ability to provide a stable and supportive environment for any child produced as a result of treatment', and 'their ages and likely future ability to provide for a child's needs'.

Private clinics are just as bound as NHS clinics to take all these factors into consideration. But while some single women, gay women and older women have been treated in private clinics, such people have very little

chance on the NHS, where budgets for IVF are tight. NHS clinics usually do not select people who are over 40, or even in their late 30s, and who are not part of a stable heterosexual couple.

A source close to Jack Straw, the home secretary, said that ministers had always anticipated that the new act would have implications for all departments, and stressed that all new policy was 'tested' to ensure that it was consistent with the European convention on human rights. However, he said it would be up to the courts to decide on cases in which new rights established under the human rights act appeared to clash with UK rules on fertility. 'The act will obviously result in a lot of test cases,' he said, but 'the nature and the beauty of the convention is that it is about balancing rights.'

Baroness Warnock, who chaired the 1984 committee of inquiry into human fertilisation and embryology, and is an adviser on medical ethics to the Archbishop of Canterbury, described the law as 'a real can of worms'.

'It never seemed to me the right to a family enshrined in European law had any reference to single people, post-menopausal women or homosexual couples,' she said. 'It seems to me to be very risky to interpret the law in that way.'

Diane Blood, who won the right to be artificially inseminated with her dead husband's sperm, and gave birth to her son in December 1998 after a four-year legal battle, said: 'As far as my understanding of the law goes, people already have those rights but they have to go to Strasbourg to get them enforced. This is just bringing the right within the domestic law, instead of them having to fight an expensive legal battle.'

Peter Tatchell, of the gay rights campaign group Outrage!, said: 'All the unjustified restrictions will have to be abolished. It's good that these previously overlooked issues are now to be acknowledged by European jurisprudence.'

Babies borne by men 'possible'

By Jane Hughes

Advances in medical science mean that it is now technically possible for men to bear children, according to Britain's leading fertility expert, Professor Lord Winston.

Lord Winston, a pioneer of in-vitro fertilisation techniques, says in a new book that an embryo could be implanted in a man's abdomen – with the placenta attached to an internal organ such as the bowel – and later delivered by Caesarean section. However, other experts expressed serious misgivings about the treatment, saying the chances of a successful pregnancy were extremely low and needed to be balanced against the risks to the man's health.

The prospect of male pregnancy, fictionalised in the film *Junior* starring Arnold Schwarzenegger, is raised in Lord Winston's book, *The IVF Revolution*, published in April. 'It would be technically possible for a man to bear a child,' said the professor, head of the fertility clinic at Hammersmith Hospital in west London and presenter of the BBC television series *The Human Body*.

He acknowledged that such a technique would involve treating the man with female hormones and could be dangerous because of the risk of bleeding.

The male pregnancy would imitate an ectopic pregnancy in a woman, a condition where the embryo begins to develop outside the uterus and which can prove fatal.

According to Dr Gillian Lockwood, a clinical research fellow at the John Radcliffe hospital in Oxford, male pregnancy would be theoretically viable but the chances of success would be 'thousands to one against'.

In addition to the feminising side-effects of hormonal treatment,

In theory, the technique could allow homosexual couples to have children and help heterosexual couples where the woman cannot carry a child

Dr Lockwood says, the man would also need a partial colostomy because the placenta would not come away cleanly. 'The lining of the womb is specially designed to allow the placenta to invade it and come away freely when the baby is born,' she said. 'No other organ in the body can do this and without the protective uterine muscle the baby runs a real risk of being damaged.

'Even when we transfer embryos into the uterus there is only a 50-50 chance of them becoming attached, so the chance of getting an embryo to stick in the wrong place is very low.'

Doctors would have to obtain permission to carry out the treatment from the Human Fertilisation and Embryology Authority. A spokesman for the authority said applications would be subjected to a rigorous assessment process that would consider the reasons behind the treatment as well as its safety and effectiveness.

In theory, the technique could allow homosexual couples to have children and help heterosexual couples where the woman cannot carry a child.

ADDITIONAL RESOURCES

You might like to contact the following organisations for further information. Due to the increasing cost of postage, many organisations cannot respond to enquiries unless they receive a stamped, addressed envelope.

British Humanist Association (BHA)
47 Theobald's Road
London, WC1X 8SP
Tel: 020 7430 0908
Fax: 020 7430 1271
E-mail: info@humanism.org.uk
Web site: www.humanism.org.uk
The British Humanist Association is the UK's leading organisation for people concerned with ethics and society, free from religious and supernatural dogma. It represents, supports and serves humanists in the United Kingdom and is a registered charity with more than fifty affiliated local groups. Publishes a wide range of free briefings including the issues of racism, discrimination and prejudice, abortion, euthanasia and surrogacy.

British Medical Association (BMA)
BMA House
Tavistock Square
London, WC1H 9JP
Tel: 020 7387 4499
Fax: 020 7383 6400
E-mail: enquiries@bma.org.uk
Web site: www.bma.org.uk
The British Medical Association is a professional association of doctors, representing their interests and providing services for its 122,000 plus members.

Centre for Reproductive Medicine
4 Priory Road
Clifton
Bristol, BS8 1TY
Tel: 0117 902 1100
Fax: 0117 902 1101
E-mail: admin@ReproMED.co.uk
Web site: www.repromed.co.uk
The University of Bristol's Centre for Reproductive Medicine was founded in 1983 on the clear principle that the best possible clinical services to diagnose and treat infertile couples should run hand in hand with basic research to better understand the causes of infertility.

Christian Medical Fellowship (CMF)
157 Waterloo Road
London, SE1 8XN
Tel: 020 7928 4694
Fax: 020 7620 2453
E-mail: admin@cmf.org.uk
Web site: www.cmf.org.uk
A network of approximately 4,500 doctors and 600 medical students throughout the UK and Republic of Ireland. They produce a range of booklets and leaflets, including CMF files.

fpa (formerly The Family Planning Association)
2-12 Pentonville Road
London, N1 9FP
Tel: 020 7837 5432
Fax: 020 7837 3042
Web site: www.fpa.org.uk
fpa produces information and publications on all aspects of reproduction and sexual health – phone for a publications catalogue. The Helpline on 020 7837 4044 Monday-Friday 9am to 7pm is run by qualified healthcare workers and can answer queries on all aspects of family planning.

ISSUE – The National Fertility Association
114 Lichfield Street
Walsall, WS1 1SZ
Tel: 01922 722888
Fax: 01922 640070
E-mail: webmaster@issue.co.uk
Web site: www.issue.co.uk
Provides help, information, support and representation to people with fertility difficulties and those who work with them. Callers are answered 24 hours a day. Confidential telephone counselling by qualified counsellors is available to all every weekday evening. Produces publications.

LIFE
LIFE House
Newbold Terrace
Leamington Spa
Warwickshire, CV32 4EA
Tel: 01926 421587
Fax: 01926 336497
E-mail: info@lifeuk.org
Web site: www.lifeuk.org
LIFE provides a nationwide care service for pregnant girls and women – as well as for unsupported mothers, women with problems relating to pregnancy, fertility or infertility, or suffering from the effects of abortion. It is not a religious orgnaisation.

PPP healthcare
Phillip House
Crescent Road
Tunbridge Wells, TN1 2PL
Tel: 01892 512345
Fax: 01892 515143
Web site: www.ppphealthcare.co.uk
PPP healthcare is one of the UK's leading private healthcare companies. Health Information Line 0800 003 004.

The Progress Educational Trust
140 Grays Inn Road
London, WC1X 8AX
Tel: 020 7278 7870
Fax: 020 7278 7868
E-mail: admin@progress.org.uk
Web site: www.progress.org.uk
PROGRESS is made up of organisations and individuals who have come together to support and protect controlled research into the earliest stages of human development and the prevention of infertility, miscarriage and congenital handicap. Produce factsheets, reports and a newsletter.

INDEX

*****

The Internet has been likened to shopping in a supermarket without aisles. The press of a button on a Web browser can bring up thousands of sites but working your way through them to find what you want can involve long and frustrating on-line searches.

And unfortunately many sites contain inaccurate, misleading or heavily biased information. Our researchers have therefore undertaken an extensive analysis to bring you a selection of quality Web site addresses.

fpa (formerly The Family Planning Association)
www.fpa.org.uk
fpa (formerly The Family Planning Association) is the only registered charity working to improve the sexual health and reproductive rights of all people throughout the UK. An extensive and informative site.

ISSUE – The National Fertility Association
www.issue.co.uk
ISSUE provides a totally confidential comprehensive service which includes factsheets, information, support, counselling and literature on infertility and reproductive health.

Centre for Reproductive Medicine
www.repromed.co.uk]
This web site is for anyone in the UK interested in reproductive medicine. Click on Fertility Information for a vast amount of relevant information on fertility issues.

Human Fertilisation & Embryology Authority (HFEA)
www.hfea.gov.uk
Click on the Patient Information button. The HFEA's 'Patient Information' pages aim to help people who are considering IVF, Donor Insemination, ICSI, or GIFT with donated sperm or eggs to understand the services offered by licensed clinics, to decide which treatment would be the best for them and to give advice on how to choose a clinic.

Christian Medical Fellowship (CMF)
www.cmf.org.uk
CMF produces information addressing a wide range of ethical issues from a Christian perspective. The Site Index provides links to articles on numerous ethical topics. Or click on the Ethics button. This takes you to the link for Infertility Treatments and Reproductive Technologies.

ACKNOWLEDGEMENTS

The publisher is grateful for permission to reproduce the following material.

While every care has been taken to trace and acknowledge copyright, the publisher tenders its apology for any accidental infringement or where copyright has proved untraceable. The publisher would be pleased to come to a suitable arrangement in any such case with the rightful owner.

Chapter One: An Introduction

What can cause infertility?, © fpa, *Causes of infertility*, © National Infertility Awareness Campaign (NIAC), *Male infertility*, © PPP healthcare, 2000, *Female infertility*, © PPP healthcare, 2000, *Fertility myths*, © Professor William Ledger MA, *More couples beat infertility*, © Telegraph Group Limited, London 2000, *Fertility laws*, © Guardian Newspapers Limited, 2000.

Chapter Two: Treatment and Options

Fertility – introduction, © 2000 Centre for Reproductive Medicine, Bristol, UK, *The treatment methods*, © 2000 Centre for Reproductive Medicine, Bristol, UK, *One in five treatments are a success*, © The Independent, November 1999, *In-vitro fertilisation*, © ISSUE, *New egg fusion technique*, © Progress Educational Trust, *Surrogacy – fact and opinion*, © LIFE, *Surrogacy*, © ISSUE, *Considering surrogacy?*, © British Medical Association (BMA).

Chapter Three: The Ethics

Family values and fertility issues, © British Humanist Association (BHA), *Infertility*, © Christian Medical Fellowship (CMF), *The death of natural procreation*, © LIFE, *A dangerous path*, © Professor Anthony O'Hear, *'Faceless fathers' may be identified*, © The Independent, April 2000, *Should sperm donors be traceable?*, © Guardian Newspapers Limited, 2000, *This foolish threat to the gift of life*, © Lord Robert Winston, *The battle to join the test-tube baby boom*, © The Daily Mail, February 2000, *Human rights test for fertility rules*, © Guardian Newspapers Limited, 2000, *Babies borne by men 'possible'*, © The Independent, February 1999.

Photographs and illustrations:

Pages 1, 3, 7, 8, 19, 23, 30: Pumpkin House, pages 4, 10, 21, 28, 33, 34, 36, 39: Simon Kneebone.

Craig Donnellan
Cambridge
September, 2000